401.93 MYS

D1081363

Living LANGUAGE

LANGUAGE ACQUISITION

Frank Myszor

Hodder & Stoughton

A MEMBER OF THE HODDER HEADLINE GROUP

401.93 MVS

31708
114936

Acknowledgements

Thanks to: Katharine, Ann Harris, Paul Happe, Jackie Baker, Roger Jones, Emma Hurst, Adam Healey and the students of Itchen College.

For Jacob.

Copyright Text:

pp 9–10 from *A Child's Learning of English* by Paul Fletcher, Blackwells; pp 11–12 from *Early Language* by Paul and Jill de Villiers, HarperCollins; p 15 'Reading Scheme' by Wendy Cope from *Making Cocoa for Kingsley Amis*, Faber and Faber Ltd; p 17 *Spot's First Walk* by Eric Hill, Ventura Publishing Limited; p 22 from *Invader Pre-School Series*; p 23 from *Animals at Home*, Dinosaur Publications; pp 25–26 'Adventure at the Lighthouse' from *The Rainbow Annual 1956*; p 27 *The Camcorder* from The Oxford Reading Tree, as appeared in Summer 1996 AEB English Language examination; pp 25–26 *The Big Sneeze* by Ruth Brown, Andersen Press Limited; p 31 *Baby talk important tool for learning, study says* by Lauran Neergard © Detroit Free Press; p 32 Reply to internet question by Daniel Lefkowitz, taken with permission from The Linguist List; p 39 'Monologue 1' and 'Monologue 2' from *The Mental and Social Life of Babies* by Kenneth Kaye, 1984, Methuen; p 47 from *On Becoming a Speaking Mammal* by F. Katamba, 1996, Longman; p 58 from *The Language Instinct* by Steven Pinker, 1994, Penguin Books; p 59 from *Journal of Child Language* by C. Stoel Gammon and J. A. Cooper, 1984, Cambridge University Press; pp 60–61 extract from *Natural Genius* produced by Anne McNaught, first broadcast 20/9/95, BBC Radio 4; p 74 from *Action, Gesture and Symbol: The Emergence of Language* edited by Andrew Lock, Academic Press.

Orders: please contact Bookpoint Ltd, 39 Milton Park, Abingdon, Oxon OX14 4TD. Telephone: (44) 01235 400414, Fax: (44) 01235 400454. Lines are open from 9.00–6.00, Monday to Saturday, with a 24 hour message answering service. Email address: orders@bookpoint.co.uk

British Library Cataloguing in Publication Data
A catalogue record for this title is available from The British Library

ISBN 0 340 73083 8

First published 1999
Impression number   10 9 8 7 6 5 4 3 2 1
Year   2005 2004 2003 2002 2001 2000 1999

Copyright © 1999 Frank Myszor

All rights reserved. No part of this publication may be reproduced or transmitted in any form or by any means, electronic or mechanical, including photocopy, recording, or any information storage and retrieval system, without permission in writing from the publisher or under licence from the Copyright Licensing Agency Limited. Further details of such licences (for reprographic reproduction) may be obtained from the Copyright Licensing Agency Limited, of 90 Tottenham Court Road, London W1P 9HE.

Cover photo from The Ronald Grant Archive.
Typeset by Fakenham Photosetting Limited, Fakenham, Norfolk.
Printed in Great Britain for Hodder & Stoughton Educational, a division of Hodder Headline Plc, 338 Euston Road, London NW1 3BH by Scotprint Ltd, Musselburgh, Scotland.

BARTON PEVERIL
COLLEGE LIBRARY
EASTLEIGH SO50 5ZA

CONTENTS

1 Framing Questions about Language Acquisition

'Children learn language in the first place because they strive to ... share what they and other persons are feeling and thinking'

(Lois Bloom, 1993, p 245)

The purpose of this first chapter is to introduce some of the important themes and issues in the study of children's language acquisition. We will also consider some of the linguistic problems of writing a book such as this. Above all its purpose is to establish a context for understanding language acquisition. Amidst all of the academic studies, the tables of results and the transcripts of dialogues it is worth remembering that there are real babies – real people – involved; you should therefore acquaint yourselves with one or two of the case studies of real babies on pages 7, 8, 11 and 12 before moving on to other chapters.

Asking the right questions: 'how?' means more than 'when?'

What questions do you ask first when you think about children acquiring language? For many people the first question is dominated by the word 'when?' ... 'When do babies say their first word?' ... 'When do babies first intend to say something?' A variation on this question is 'Does X happen before Y?' ... 'Do children understand things before they can say them?' ... 'Do girls learn to speak before boys?' There is a tendency in the study of child language development to emphasise such questions, as if the order in which development occurs is the most important issue. According to this view, understanding language acquisition is about understanding the order in which children learn about various aspects of speech: vocabulary, grammar, **phonology** (sounds) and **pragmatics** (rules for conversation).

This book does address this issue and there is no intention to deny its importance. But it also attempts to break the stranglehold of 'when ... before ... after?' questions and to emphasise other important questions such as: 'how?', 'which?', 'under what circumstances?' and 'why?', as in:

'How do babies learn language?' ...

'Which situations help them to speak?' ...

'Under what circumstances do children learn to take turns?' . . .

'Why do children say "runned"?' . . .

Because of this shift of emphasis, this book is not set out in accordance with the stages of language development so often described elsewhere. The point is developed later in this chapter.

Most studies of language acquisition take the child up to the age of about 5, by which time most of the features of adult language are established. The other reason for stopping at this point is that the child is turning from a primarily oral world towards one in which the printed word plays a significant part. Unusually, this book takes the next step and follows the child into that written mode of existence, a world in which the child is faced with print, alphabet, pictures, computer screens and so forth. This has been done partly for the purpose of seeing 'acquisition' in a broader perspective (that some define as 'development'), and partly because writing for young children offers interesting possibilities for analysis and original writing.

Writing about language acquisition

ACTIVITY 1

Imagine that you are about to write a textbook for A-Level students on language acquisition. Before you start you will need to make some decisions about the kind of language you will use to refer to the two or three main 'characters' in the book. Choose three or four preferred words from the list opposite and be prepared to justify your choice to a partner. For example, would you consider 'At six months the baby and his mother...' to be acceptable in a book such as this?

baby newborn tot child(ren) infant

he she they s/he he or she

parent adult caregiver mother father

COMMENTARY It may seem easy to choose three or four of these words without facing further problems. But in fact each of them presents its own difficulty, usually because of who is included or excluded from the category named by the word. 'Infant' literally means 'without speech' and so will usually be used for the earlier phases of development. Elsewhere 'baby' will be preferred and gender bias will be avoided by alternating male and female pronouns ('he' and 'she'). Grammatical purists may be shocked to find the plural form 'they' occasionally used to refer to one person. As for the adults, they will be just that, but also 'parents' depending on the best fit for the context, the other terms being either too new, too politically correct or just plain sexist! One exception to this will be where specific research deals only with, say, mothers, in which case the word used in the original research will be used.

Be aware of the implications of your choice of vocabulary as you tackle the activities in this book.

Frameworks for the study of language acquisition

Every field of study needs its guiding principles and key concepts – a kind of mental map that guides your thoughts as you seek a more detailed understanding. However, it is important that a guide does not become a straitjacket.

The process of acquiring or developing language obviously takes place through time, and so this often becomes a key concept, alongside the ages of the children being studied.

Researchers have also attempted to link ages with **stages**, which can be defined as the characteristic features of a child's language for a certain period of time, usually about one year. A stage implies a kind of plateau during which a particular aspect of language remains relatively stable; for example, the way in which the child asks questions. Usually the number of words the child can say in any one utterance is important for defining stages. This is sometimes scored as the **mean length of utterance** (**MLU**), devised by Roger Brown in 1969. It is calculated by dividing the total number of words (or **morphemes**) spoken by the number of utterances. So if a baby used two words in total and there were two utterances, the MLU would be 'one'. Brown has related MLU score to stages, as in: stage 1(MLU scores from 1.1–2.0); stage 2 (2.0–2.5); stage 3 (2.5–3.0); stage 4 (3.0–3.5); stage 5 (3.5–4.0). The principle behind this system is that the length of a baby's utterances is a good indicator of her linguistic development. A more detailed account of how to calculate MLU can be found in: *Learning to Be Literate* (1998), A. Garton and C. Pratt.

The problems with stages

Stages are useful for getting a hold on language acquisition, for charting a child's development and comparing children, but they also have their limitations.

The idea of a plateau, mentioned above, tends to flatten out complexities, suggesting that the child remains the same for the duration of a stage, and obscuring the rough edges that characterise research in this area.

Stages also tend to emphasise one kind of development to the neglect of another. For example, the definition of the one-word stage takes little account of the ways in which babies pronounce words. But why should pronunciation exactly map the path of development taken by grammar?

Stages can also put the emphasis on similarities *between* rather than differences between children, distracting us from the considerable variation that exists between individuals.

Finally, because different aspects of language progress at different rates, more and more stages are required, so you will find stages that describe children's formation of negative sentences, asking questions and even using the word 'and'! The chart below shows some of the stages that have been proposed:

Figure 1

Chart showing some of the stages of development for various features of language

```
                              Approximate Age
    _ _ _ 0 _ _ _ _ _ _ _ _ _ _ 1 _ _ _ _ _ _ _ _ _ _ _ _ 2 _ _ _ _ _ _ _ _ _ _ _ _ 3 _ _ _ _ _ _ _ _ _ _ 4+
         __pre-linguistic_____
          (phonology) p 73
S
T                                          _____Brown's MLU_p 3_____
A
G                            _____Functions/purposes of language (Halliday) p 48_____
E
                          _____vocabulary (eg Nelson 1988) pp 62, 67_____
T
H                    _____one/two word/telegraphic etc (eg Crystal 1976) pp 42–44, 64_____
E
O                                _____negatives (Bellugi 1967) p 51_____
R
I                    _____asking questions (eg Clarke 1985) p 52_____
E
S
```

As well as considering the various stages, this book will describe language development in terms of:

phonology – the characteristic pronunciations of a child

grammar – how words are combined and constructed

vocabulary/lexis – words and their meanings

pragmatics – rules for holding a conversation

These types of analysis are important because together they make up the systematic framework described in the subject criteria for English Language A-Level. In order to be successful you will need to demonstrate your ability to use these methods of analysis.

ACTIVITY 2

Design a chart for showing the advantages and disadvantages of stage theories. The chart is to be part of a general introductory book about language acquisition aimed at parents and other interested adults.

Basic assumptions about language acquisition

ACTIVITY 3

What assumptions do you make about children and the way in which they learn language? Discuss the statements below with a partner. Decide whether or not they are true.

1 Some normal babies produce no words until they are at least two years old.
2 Babies can learn to speak using the television.
3 Babies of deaf parents 'say' their first word before babies of speaking parents.
4 Language acquisition is innate so a baby locked in a room for four years with little human contact will still learn to speak.
5 Babies learn language by copying adults.
6 Babies pick up 'babytalk' from their parents.
7 Bilingual children are often slow to talk.
8 Babies who can only say two words cannot make themselves clear.
9 It matters how much you talk to your baby.
10 You can speed up children's language development.
11 At birth any child can learn any language fluently.

(Answers to Activity 3 will be found at the end of the chapter.)

How is language development studied?

There are basically two ways of studying children's language. The first is **naturalistic observation** which involves recording children speaking in natural circumstances, usually at home and sometimes over several years. The second (which could be called **controlled experiment**) encompasses a wide range of techniques but essentially seeks to control the situation to a greater or lesser extent, perhaps by asking pre-planned questions or by getting the child to play a game.

Naturalistic observation appears easy enough. But be warned! Babies can be very uncooperative, very difficult to understand and you may simply find yourself not getting the kind of data you want. Some of the pitfalls of this approach are illustrated in Activity 4 below. Controlled experiments are often better for observing a specific aspect of language. Possibilities include: giving a child utterances to imitate; playing games that require a particular language use, like forming negatives; showing the baby pictures to form plurals or passives. These techniques will be described in more detail at the appropriate places in this book. Whichever method you choose it is important that you get parents' permission and explain what you want to do.

You should also be aware of the need to evaluate different methods of studying children's language for exam purposes.

The following four extracts are taken from a student's investigation into the language of her 2 year old cousin. The purpose is to get the baby talking as much as possible in a naturalistic setting, with the student and other family members present. Extracts 1 and 2 were recorded six months after Extracts 3 and 4.

Consider in each case the problems the student faced when collecting this data. The student is C and her cousin A. All punctuation except the representation of short pauses (.) has been omitted.

Extract 1

C: who did you go with

A: um with Richard and a (.) those (.) and um (.) we have a nice time with Richard and Sa um no Sarah there

C: were they

A: no Sarah there

C: was she

A: no

Extract 2

C: did you go to the beach

A: yes

C: yes (.) what was it like

A: um cloudy [*unclear*]

C: was it cloudy

A: no cold

C: oh cold

Extract 3

C: what do you do if it's too hot

A: blow it

C: you blow it

A: wake up Danny up

C: go on then ...

Extract 4

C: where's Lucie today then ... she's up the pub

A: not pup ... no (.) Lu is at work today Lucie where Lucie is

C: is what

A: Lucie Lucie a work ...

COMMENTARY

In the first extract the student doesn't seem to have understood the child's way of saying that Sarah wasn't there and so C's next two utterances seem inappropriate. In Extract 2 there are different kinds of problems. The initial **closed question** ('did you go to the beach') gets a predictably limited response and so C tries an **open-ended question** ('what was it like'). Again there is a single-word response with the additional problem that she can't quite make it out. The third extract illustrates the problem of getting children to do what you want. Here A ignores adult rules for changing the subject by suddenly introducing a new topic – she wants to wake up Danny who is sitting there asleep. In the fourth the child's intonation must have suggested that her sentence was incomplete, so that C asks her to complete it ('is what'). The child is again faced with repeating herself and this has happened throughout the extracts, largely as a result of the student's inexperience at interpreting the child's utterances. These problems tend to limit the fruitfulness of the data which can become stilted and repetitive as a result.

Frequently asked questions

The rest of this chapter introduces you to a range of babies' language, some of the questions you might want to ask about this topic and some real babies.

Does it matter how adults talk to babies?

A Tonversation with Baby

"'Z oo sinkin' of tisses, tunnin

'N wannin 'n wannin for some?

O tweety goo swummy doodle,

O yummy yum!"

(AUTHOR NOT KNOWN)

This has become an important question for parents in recent years because academics claim that the way adults speak to babies influences development. 'Babytalk' has become recognised as a **register** of English, like foreigner talk; that is, as a variety that depends on the situation you are in and the person you are talking to. It has important implications for the role of experience as opposed to innate factors in the acquisition of language; that is, for the extent to which children learn language from others around them as opposed to being biologically 'pre-programmed' to learn it. If babies do learn from others, it is highly likely that adult 'babytalk' will play an important part. This will be covered in chapter 3.

ACTIVITY 5

1 Describe the language of the quotation from 'A Tonversation with Baby' in terms of phonology and vocabulary.
2 In a small group brainstorm the features you think are typical of the way adults talk to babies. What effect might use of this language have on babies' development?

When do babies start to learn language?

Case Study 1 – Jacob

The extract below is from a father's diary beginning a few days after the birth of his son.

Within a few days of being born Jacob can stick out his tongue in response to the same from his parents (father actually), albeit with a delay of a few seconds. He looks around frequently and has done this from the moment of his birth, particularly at lights, (and as he was born shortly before Christmas there are plenty to attract him) although he would have been unable to focus on anything further than a foot from his face.

At three weeks there have been no smiles. Easily the most noticeable feature of his behaviour is his crying. The crying of such a young baby is apparently differentiated according to its driving force – usually the discomfort caused by a soiled nappy or hunger for his mother's milk. However, this is often difficult to distinguish on the basis of the cry alone and we are often forced to assume that he must need feeding.

After two and a half weeks of life Jacob develops colic, basically a windy stomach (just like his father!), a complaint common in babies. From then on his cries seem to become more frequent and more piercing. The cry of a three week old baby is intense and shrill, sometimes like the painful sound of a tomcat fighting at night, and when it really hots up it suddenly develops a kind of vibrato, a sharp throaty wobble as it hits its peak. It is both painful to hear and is clearly triggered by pain. At the moment I still cannot link these variations with their precise causes.

The textbooks say that he should be able to recognise his parents after a few weeks and this is confirmed to some extent by the fact of Jacob's crying immediately becoming more subdued as soon as he is put into his mother's arms. But I wonder if it's just an animal response to the smell of milk? At around this time (3–4 weeks) he deliberately turns his head and looks around, wide-eyed. When he is not crying he seems to make other noises that sometimes resemble the soft twittering of birds.

At around five weeks smiling is surely imminent. I keep seeing half smiles and potential smirks. It's becoming frustrating. Sometimes I think he is picking up the basics of turn-taking – if you talk to him with exaggerated intonation, perhaps asking a question, he seems to open his mouth as if attempting to say something. But this is surely only copying what he sees. I doubt very much that he intends to communicate. His legs are becoming noticeably stronger so that he pushes himself up when he is sitting on your lap. Still can't distinguish the functions of cries: I only know that some are more painful than others.

First smile claimed at five weeks, six days. Over a period of a few days I suddenly see a more expressive face, eyes that look more, a head that turns more and limbs that kick more. Noises are becoming more varied: sometimes they sound like 'ow' but you wouldn't yet call them attempts at words and neither is there any sense of his shaping his mouth in any deliberate way. Soon he is able to hit out at plastic objects attached to the bar above his cot.

By nine weeks interaction with Jacob is a lot more satisfying. He regularly moves his lips when you talk to him. When you touch his nose he holds his mouth open in a kind of laugh and you can begin to play a game in which you repeatedly touch his nose and he reacts the same way every time. For the first time I've seen him rub his eye with his hand.

At twelve weeks, amazingly, he can hold his rattle and bring it up to his mouth to suck.

(the author, Dec 1997– Feb 1998)

ACTIVITY 6

1 If you are carrying out an investigation/project involving a young child write a profile using notes collected from the parents. If possible try to keep your own diary on a young baby and use this as the basis for follow-up research on one of the issues covered in this book.

2 Re-read the diary extract and discuss these questions:

   a Is it true to say that Jacob has no

language? Pick out anything which you think will help him to learn.

b Do you think that babies have different kinds of cries? If so, is this language?

COMMENTARY

Undoubtedly Jacob is learning some of the building blocks of language, if not language itself. In particular, his ability to copy movements of the tongue and mouth (which seems to be associated with sounds coming from others), his apparent turn-taking, his enjoyment of a repeated activity. Crying communicates but it is not language. The different kinds can be distinguished by some parents (but not this one). Crying is a reflex reaction to a particular stimulus, and although it varies we can hardly say that there is an intention to communicate.

This account raises issues connected with exactly when a baby starts to learn language. Most of the early research was concerned with the baby's first words. It wasn't until more sophisticated equipment was developed that researchers were able to study how much babies could understand before they had produced their first words. Most experts now agree on a sequence of stages that take the baby roughly from crying to babbling, although they sometimes describe it in slightly different ways. The most recent developments explore pre-natal learning about language – there is growing evidence that some things about language are learned before birth.

What can a two year old say?

Below are two samples from the speech of two two year olds. Sophie is the third daughter of a middle class family living in the south of England. She first started to speak at the age of 14 months. Katharine is the first daughter of middle class parents. At the time of recording Sophie was 28 months and Katharine 27 months old.

ACTIVITY 7

Compare the following two transcripts. Which child is the more advanced linguistically? In the first place use your intuitions about language but then attempt a more systematic approach. Take into account grammar, phonology, vocabulary, pragmatics (what part do the babies play in the conversation?) and comprehension. Calculate the MLU for each one (see page 3).

Transcription code: pauses are indicated by a number in brackets; where pronunciation is non-standard this is shown in the spelling; conventional punctuation is used.
If you have the cassette tape that accompanies this book you will also be able to listen to Katharine's dialogue (Tape Extract 1).

Sophie

S: You take your bissies.

F: I've eaten them.

S: Me want more bissies.

F: No, you've had one of mine.

S: Me want nother bissie.

F: Well you'll have one later.

S: No. Mary come me. Only little bit.

F: Not today cos it's Wednesday.

S: Why? Jack come.

F: No. They came yesterday.

S: [*5 syllable indecipherable utterance*]

F: Where did you put it?

S: Over there. No.

F: Would you like to tidy up the doll's house?

S: Where [*1 syllable*] go? Where's the doll's house?

F: Here on the floor. Shall we put this away?

S: No.

(adapted from Fletcher,1985, Blackwells)

Katharine (Tape Extract 1)

K: We do Jason again shall we?

M: What, draw another picture of Jason?

K: Yeh

M: Mmm yeh, we could do . . . what else could we do a picture of? Ooh! That's a good one. Is that the head?

K: Now I'll do Jason.

M: Mmhu.

K: I'll do his head first. He's at de top of the circle.

M: Uhuh.

K: Dere he is.

M: Oh that's very good.

K: Dat's his head.

M: Uhuh. Where's his body?

K: [*makes noise*] Dere's his legs, touching his mouf.

M: Touching his mouth? Do your legs touch your mouth?

K: No they don't.

M: What comes in between? (1) What's in between your mouth and the tops of your legs?

K: Yeh.

M: What's this bit?

K: I dunno.

M: You do. It's the rest of your body, isn't it? Your chest and . . . [*pats stomach*]

K: Tummy.

M: Yes.

COMMENTARY This is clear evidence of the varied abilities of children of the same age. One of the findings that will recur throughout this book is that children develop at different speeds even though the course of their development will have much in common. Here, Katharine's grammar is more complex, more varied and it shows more use of appropriate forms. For example, 'We do Jason again, shall we?' shows the use of subject, verb, object, adverbial followed by a tag question. Later she varies this by changing the pronoun to 'I', using the future tense ('I'll') and brings the adverbial to the beginning of the sentence ('now') in 'Now I'll do Jason' (although it is debatable whether she says 'I'll' or 'I'). Whereas Sophie uses the object pronoun 'me' at the beginnings of sentences ('Me want more bissies'), Katharine uses 'I' as well as a variety of other pronouns.

How do children learn to speak so well in such a short time?

Consider some of the extraordinary facts of language acquisition:

1 All children learn to speak within a few years unless brain damaged.
2 Very few parents are trained to accomplish this task.
3 Babies are given no or little explicit instruction to help them.
4 Babies hear only a limited sample of language whilst they learn it.
5 Babies produce sentences they have never heard anyone say.
6 Few other animals are capable of much language at all.
7 There are no gaps in between words in spoken language: babies hear a continuous stream of sound.
8 If you expose a baby to two languages at the same time they will learn both.

ACTIVITY 8

Discuss in a small group how theories might be able to explain these findings. Which statements suggest that language is mainly innate (biologically pre-programmed) and which that it is learned from the environment?

Can babies learn to speak from television?

Case Study 2 – Jim Jim was a hearing child whose parents were both profoundly deaf. The following study was reported by De Villiers and De Villiers:

The parents had only a few words of oral speech and used sign language to each other, but they knew that Jim could hear so they thought it inappropriate to use sign language with him. He therefore saw adults sign to each other but had only rudimentary gestures directed towards him by his parents. Under these conditions he learned no formal sign language, just a few gestures. Jim had little contact with other children or speaking adults but he watched television frequently, so most of the language he learned came from television programmes. He heard only the occasional single word utterance from his parents. Jim was two and a half before he tried to use language, at which point he produced a few words, most of them taken from television jingles. At the age of three years and nine months he came to the attention of speech therapists and researchers, and his language skills were extensively tested. Jim fell well below his age level on standard tests of linguistic ability, and in several respects his language differed from that of children with normal language development. The intonation pattern of his utterances was abnormally flat, communicating little effect. Although he tried to communicate concepts appropriate to the situation he was talking about, he lacked the necessary knowledge of English grammar, so his sentences possessed a very idiosyncratic structure ...

After regular therapy sessions, Jim showed dramatic improvement in his speech. In one month he progressed a full year in age level on standard tests, and at four years and two months his mastery of English grammar was typical for his age group.

(De Villiers and De Villiers, 1979, Fontana Paperbacks)

ACTIVITY 9

At three years and nine months Jim was able to say the utterances listed below. How does his language compare with that of normal children? You might like to compare it with the two two year olds above. Consider: the number of words he can combine and the order in which he links them (compare this with the conventional adult order); the way in which he forms words (**morphology**).

1 House. Two houses. Not one house. That two house.
2 Not window. Two window.
3 That enough two wing.
4 Two crayon. Big two crayon.

5 My mommy my house a play ball.
6 My mommy in the house apple.
7 House chimney. My house my chimney.
8 Fall that back.
9 Be down go.
10 There crash it.
11 That car it go truck.
12 Go downstairs snack.
13 Off my mittens.
14 Not broke that.
15 This not take off plane.
16 Right there wheels.
17 Going house a fire truck.
18 Where is it plane.

COMMENTARY

Clearly Jim's case shows how an extreme situation can disrupt the normal course of development, suggesting that interaction with speaking people is essential. In this case Jim is a little behind the average three year old: he sometimes fails to add plural endings and there are considerable problems with word order.

> ### Answers to Activity 3
> 1 This is true. There is considerable variation in the speed and manner in which children learn language. Some children do not say much for the first two years but when they do start speaking it is obvious that a lot of learning has been taking place.
> 2 No. You can pick up some vocabulary from television but it lacks the interactive dimension. See the case study of Jim on pages 11–12.
> 3 This is often true. Signing words is generally easier than

articulating them and so deaf babies are not slowed down by problems of articulation in the early stages of speaking.

4   Not true. Although many psychologists regard some aspects of language acquisition as being innate, exposure to language is still necessary in order to learn.

5   Only true to a limited extent, as much of the research of the last 40 years has shown.

6   No. Babytalk was started by babies! Adult versions reflect the way that babies speak and to some extent adults will teach their children this 'language'.

7   Yes. Acquiring two languages at the same time does tend to slow down the rate of acquisition.

8   No. Adults are very skilful at making the most of limited information, often using the context to clarify what the baby has said.

9   Yes. Babies whose parents talk to them more learn to speak faster.

10   If the above is true then this one must also be. There are a number of ways in which adults speak to babies that are associated with more rapid development. But there are no miraculous hot-housing techniques.

11   True. There are no in-built constraints on which language can be learned.

This chapter introduced the study of children's language acquisition. It described some of the frameworks and methods that researchers have used, warning against the rigidity of using any one stage theory. It introduced important and popular questions about language development, considering babies of different ages and in different circumstances. In a field that can become obsessed by the detailed study of parts of language it is important to remember that babies are people, not just data!

Recommended reading

The Cambridge Encyclopedia of Language, David Crystal, 1997, CUP.

Child Language, Learning and Linguistics, David Crystal, 1976, Edward Arnold.

Listen to Your Child, David Crystal, 1986, Penguin Books.

Talking and Your Child, Clare Shaw, 1993, Hodder and Stoughton.

2 Writing for Young Children

'The principal symbolic system to which the pre-school child has access is oral language.'

Margaret Donaldson (1978) p 89.

This chapter aims to consider writing for four to seven year olds, and here the emphasis will be on fiction. We will see that writers have to think very carefully about the oral abilities of their target readers.

Experts advise us to read to children almost as soon as they can speak and perhaps before. Parents are likely to read aloud and point whilst their baby looks at the pictures and helps turn over the pages. The role of such non-verbal behaviour in helping the emergence of first words suggests how important books for babies can be (see chapter 7). You will probably be familiar with some well-known stories for this age group and perhaps think they are typically short, simple and easy to write. This, unfortunately, is definitely not the case: writers for children have to think carefully about the oral abilities of the target readers and what it means for the child to move from a world with no written words in it to one created entirely by the written words on the page. In doing this they will be thinking about the content and theme, how words and sentences are combined, choice of vocabulary, as well as developing the child's language.

Children's books are written to entertain but also to educate: not just about the world but about language itself and this will influence the way that they are designed. Here we will consider both so-called '**real books**' and **reading schemes**. The former will be dealt with later in the chapter. The latter refers to series of books for children that are specially designed to teach reading as well as entertain. For this reason they are read in a fixed sequence, gradually increasing in complexity. In recent years they have been the centre of controversy and are therefore likely to get primary school teachers arguing. The controversy has concerned whether or not reading schemes are better for children's reading than 'real books'. This can make for interesting investigative projects:

■ you can compare different kinds of scheme, either produced by different publishers or based on different theories of reading instruction;
■ you can compare books aimed at readers of different ages;
■ a single text can be analysed for its gender representation.

Some well-known schemes are: *All Aboard! The Oxford Reading Tree;*
Longman Book Project; Cambridge Reading.

ACTIVITY 10

Find books from reading schemes that use two different approaches, for example, *Look and Say* (which emphasises word shapes and the context provided by pictures) and **phonics** (which emphasises sound-letter relationships). Examine the books carefully to see if there is any systematic difference in the vocabulary used.

ACTIVITY 11

Wendy Cope's poem shows how familiar we are with old-fashioned reading schemes. What features of reading schemes does Wendy Cope draw on in the poem?

Reading Scheme

Here is Peter. Here is Jane. They like fun.

Jane has a big doll. Peter has a ball.

Look, Jane, look! Look at the dog! See him run!

Here is mummy. She has baked a bun.

Here is the milkman. He has come to call.

Here is Peter. Here is Jane. They like fun.

Go Peter! Go Jane! Come, milkman come!

The milkman likes Mummy. She likes them all.

Look, Jane, look! Look at the dog! See him run!

Here are the curtains. They shut out the sun.

Let us peep! On tiptoe Jane! You are small!

Here is Peter. Here is Jane. They like fun.

I hear a car Jane. The milkman looks glum.

Here is Daddy in his car. Daddy is tall.

Look, Jane, look! Look at the dog! See him run!

Daddy looks very cross. Has he a gun?

Up milkman! Up milkman! Over the wall!

Here is Peter. Here is Jane. They like fun.

Look, Jane, look! Look at the dog! See him run!

■ Write your own poem in the style of a book from a reading scheme.

The aim of this chapter is to consider writing for young children in two ways: as texts for analysis, as in the above example, where the text probably will not be a good model for your own writing (unless you wish to write a similar kind of parody to Wendy Cope's); secondly, as a kind of writing that you could produce yourself.

ACTIVITY 12

Collect a variety of books for young children. Investigate their typical features by drawing up a list. What assumptions do you make about your readers?

From spoken to written mode

Children's first books can be seen as a kind of bridge between the child's oral world and the world of print.

ACTIVITY 13

Imagine that you are a child of about four years old. For you, language has been something you use when talking with people, you use it when people are present, it gets things done (you can ask questions or give commands) and when you have used it, it is gone! What might strike you about the written word the first time you encounter it? How will it be different from or the same as spoken language? Write down as many differences as you can think of. Consider the forms that speech and writing take; the relationship between the **addresser** and **addressee** (speaker and listener and writer and reader in each case).

COMMENTARY   You should have considered the following points:

- Spoken language does not take up physical space whereas written language does, moving from left to right and from top to bottom.
- Line breaks in writing do not affect the meaning (unless it is poetry). Pauses in spoken language do affect the meaning.
- Written language is repeatable in its exact form.
- It is permanent.
- It is non-interactive (it won't respond to your questions).
- It is separate from its addresser.

(based on Baker and Freebody, 1989)

These differences between speech and writing mean that adults have to ease children into the world of writing in a gentle way. Here are some of the features of spoken language that can be transferred to children's books:

direct speech   people in face to face interaction
narration sounding like speech   use of noises   interactive text
everyday content   use of repetition

ACTIVITY 14

Find examples of the above features in the children's books you collected earlier.

ACTIVITY 15

Analyse the picture book, *Spot's First Walk* for its oral qualities. It will also help if you are familiar with some of the differences between speech and writing. How does this book attempt to teach about language as well as entertain?

Spot's First Walk
(the book contains flaps on each page that the reader is invited to lift)

		Verbal context	Visual context
p1	*Off you go, Spot! Don't get lost.*	(Spot's Mum)	
p2	*Not in there, Spot.*	(snail replies 'Hello!')	Spot looks behind a fence
p3	*Watch Out!*	(spoken by a crow)	Spot looks in a shed
p4	*What's in the hutch, Spot?*	(hen says, 'Have a nice day!')	
p5	*That's a funny noise . . .*	(*tap . . . tap . . . tap* from tree)	Spot looks up tree
p6	*. . . and that's a nice smell*	(bee replies '*Thank you*')	Spot looks behind a gate
p7	*Are you hungry, Spot?*	(rabbit says '*Look in the flower bed*')	Spot near vegetable patch
p8	*What have you found?*	(bone)	Digging in flower bed
p9	*Now for a drink.*	(fish says '*Don't fall in*')	Next to pond
p10	*Poor Spot! Time to go home.*		Spot has fallen in
p11	*What have you been doing, Spot?*	(Spot's Mum) (Spot replies '*Not a lot*')	

COMMENTARY There is a great deal of linguistic interest in this apparently simple story. On the first page the voice is that of Spot's parent. It takes the form of a **directive** ('Off you go, Spot') followed by a mild warning (not to get lost) and it is addressed directly to Spot. There are no **speech tags** such as 'said Spot's Mum' and this continues throughout. The effect of this is that nothing gets in the way of the 'here and now' quality of the text. On the second page the words 'not in there, Spot' respond to the picture so you have to see the picture in order to fully understand the words. The language is therefore **context dependent** ('there' is **deictic**). The clipped sentence – it does not say 'Don't go in there, Spot' – underlines the closeness of the text to real speech. Underneath the flap the snail's greeting ('"Hello"') shows language being used interactively in a face to face situation.

On page three Spot is seen just about to enter a shed and a crow is warning him to 'watch out!'. 'Not in there, Spot' and 'Watch out' are written with authority, the first informing and the second warning, both showing that the voice already knows what Spot will discover. The next page asks Spot a question, prompting the reader to suggest an answer before lifting the flap of the rabbit hutch. In this respect the text teaches the question/answer **adjacency pair**, allowing the child to guess the answer from the context.

ACTIVITY 16

1 *Spot's First Walk* is highly interactive, prompting readers to lift flaps with Spot; it sounds very much like real speech; it uses direct speech; and it teaches children to predict patterns of language through its use of repetition. Continue the analysis of the book using the above as a model.
2 Write your own book with lift up flaps using some of the ideas in *Spot's First Walk* as a model. Use language with a variety of functions (inform, enquire, warn, persuade, etc); use several adjacency pairs; ally your language closely with the spoken mode; vary the purpose of lifting the flap and its contents; create more than one reason for turning the page (eg to answer a question or find out why a warning has been given); above all, create a pattern that allows the young reader to predict.

The influence of the oral tradition

The oral tradition isn't the same as the oral mode. It refers to ways of telling stories that date back to times when most people could not read and write. Before stories were written down, the language used to tell them had to be memorable so that people could learn them off by heart and re-tell them. For example, repetition plays an important part in this. The few words put before the name of a character are known as an **epithet**, as in 'fleet-footed Hermes'. The repetition of an epithet gave listeners something more to remember Hermes by than just his name.

Features borrowed from the oral tradition

Children's literature can borrow a number of specific linguistic devices from the oral tradition. You may already be familiar with many of these from studying literature:

1 **Alliteration**. This involves repetition of the same consonant or consonant cluster sound (a group of consonants together like *ch* or *gr*). For example: <u>Tr</u>eehorn's <u>Tr</u>easure (Florence Parry Heide, Puffin, 1984).
2 **Repeated epithet**. This is like an additional name tag, often an adjective that goes in front of a character's name, eg Little Mo; Little Red Riding Hood.
3 **Balanced sentence**. This occurs when two ideas are placed side by side with the second complementing, contrasting with or completing the first, eg 'Dennis didn't like the night time, didn't want to be alone.'
                                                            (*Dennis the Dragon*, Ladybird, 1980).
4 **Assonance**. Repetition of the same vowel sound, for example:

'One <u>night</u>, when she had been

put to bed <u>while</u> it was still <u>light</u>,

she made a wish.'
                                          (*A Lion in the Night*, Pamela Allen, 1985, Hamish Hamilton)

5 **Repeated formulae.** This could, for example, be a repeated spell or sequence of events.

" 'Good grief!' said the goose.

'Well, well!' said the pig.

'Who cares?' said the sheep.

'So what?' said the horse.

'What next?' said the cow."

This is repeated five times before it is finally varied in *Hattie and the Fox* by Mem Fox, Hodder and Stoughton (1988).

6 **Proverb or aphorism.** This is a saying or a summary of some accepted wisdom. For example: 'Never talk to strangers'.

7 **Parallel sentences.** This is similar to a balanced sentence except that here there is some repetition of the syntax (the grammatical structure) of the sentence. For example: 'The pianist was annoyed. The bandleader was unhappy.'

(Story Time for Four Year Olds, 1984, Ladybird)

8 **Rhythmic language.** This is best appreciated when the text is read aloud. It doesn't necessarily refer to regular rhythms but emphasises some words over others, often using a combination of alliteration and parallel sentences. See 'Comprehension of Sounds' on p 76.

9 **Epithet as metaphor.** Some epithets combine with other words to create new ways of looking at familiar ideas. For example, the expression 'whale road' to mean 'sea'. To some extent this is like children's creativity with language when they don't know the single word for something. For example, on seeing fog for the first time a child said: 'Everything's been rubbed out.'

10 **Additive structure.** The events of the story will tend to be linked using 'and' and 'but' rather than more complex structures using words such as 'because', 'therefore', 'if' etc.

For example: 'Rata was only three, but she often went to school.'

(Hemi's Pet by De Hamel and Ross)

ACTIVITY 17

Investigate the influence of the oral tradition using about six books for young children.

1 Compare how frequently the above features are used and suggest why some features are more popular than others amongst writers of children's books. Develop a tally chart for showing overall patterns but also explain particular examples.

2 Consider the possible purposes for using these techniques, for example, entertainment, attention holding, education about the world or about language, etc. For example, aphorism might be used to teach children about the world or morality; alliteration arguably increases the entertainment value of a text but also perhaps helps to hold attention.

3 Compare the ways that different kinds of books for children use features derived from the oral tradition, eg fiction v. non-fiction; books for younger and slightly older readers; etc.

4 Carry out an analysis of one or two books and how they use a range of these features. Look closely at the contexts in which they are used. Be sure to comment on how the features combine in the book as a whole.

Readability

Readability is nothing to do with a child's reading ability. It refers to how readable or unreadable a text is, which features make it more difficult, which features make it easier. Obviously a crucial factor in writing a book for children will be making sure that the text is suitable for its readers in terms of the complexity of the language. Readability can actually be measured using various mathematical formulae but here we will be more concerned with applying grammatical rules to children's books (including reading schemes) rather than measuring the readability of any particular text. Also bear in mind that a readable text isn't necessarily a good one as there are other factors that need to be taken into account.

Here, four main factors will be under consideration:

- vocabulary
- linking sentences
- constructing sentences
- lineation (mainly how the lines are organised).

Vocabulary

Some guides to writing for children recommend that you use only words of one syllable and explain everything in detail in case your readers don't understand. This is, of course, far from true. A useful rule of thumb is to keep the language relatively informal, not because young children particularly like informal language, but for the following reasons:

- An informal text is more likely to use phrasal verbs (sometimes called multi-word verbs) and so avoid more difficult words often derived from Latin. For example: 'to look down on' instead of 'to patronise'; 'to put up with' instead of 'to tolerate'.
- Informal texts are less abstract. Stories for young children should use concrete nouns in the main.
- An informal text is also likely to be closer to speech, which is, as we have seen, a desirable quality for these readers. However, representing spontaneous speech with too much realism is not a good idea. Elements of ritual and formula will tend to reduce the level of the realism.

Imagery and predictability

In the activity on page 16 you probably recommended keeping vocabulary simple and familiar to your audience. But this is not always true. More general but familiar words like 'car' and 'boat' leave open the question of what type is being referred to and therefore reduce the richness of the imagery. This also makes it more difficult to predict what will happen next, compared with, say, 'mini' or 'submarine'. The presence of pictures may of course provide this richness so you will need to consider the effects of three factors:

- the likely familiarity of the word to your readers
- the imagery it triggers off
- the relationship between the words and the pictures.

The sound of words

ACTIVITY 18

Vocabulary cannot be chosen without considering sound qualities such as:

1 Consistency of spelling and pronunciation. It is better for a book to use 'head' and 'dead' than 'head' and 'said'. Explain why and in pairs make up as many other examples as you can think of.
2 How would the words in the following sentence normally be stressed?

   We went to the park to see the birds.

   Unskilled readers often fail to create rhythmic stress patterns, putting the same stress on every word in a monotonous sounding way. If the text contains only **monosyllabic** (words with only one syllable) words as in the example above it tends to emphasise this weakness. If however, some **polysyllabic** (words with more than one syllable) words are used (like 'parrot' or 'donkey') it tends to give rhythm to the sentence as these words carry a stress pattern that the child probably already uses.

3 Make up examples of mixed monosyllabic and polysyllabic sentences (with rhyme) that you might use in a children's book. Mark on the stress patterns. Try the following topics: a parrot meets a clown; a child who can't sleep at night; animals that understand better than humans; children's fears.

Linking sentences

Another issue concerning vocabulary is the extent to which the writer:

- repeats the same noun
- replaces nouns with a pronoun
- uses a different noun for the same thing (**re-lexicalisation**).

ACTIVITY 19

In these two texts, replace the blanks with one of the three options listed above. Discuss the implications of these options for the reader. Answers can be found on page 29.

Page	At the Seaside	At School
1	Catherine is going to play with her friends on the beach.	The children take off their coats when____ arrive at school.
2	Now____has caught a starfish in her fishing net.	____do some painting first.
3	____put on their swimming rings and play in the sea.	Then____do some exercises in the gym.
4	____have a picnic in the shade of the umbrella.	Now it is breaktime.____drink milk and have something to eat.
5	____have built a big sandcastle.	____play ball in the playground.
6	____play hide and seek in the sand dunes.	Then ____watch a puppet show.

(Source: *Invader Pre-School Series* – lineation is the original)

COMMENTARY

Writers need to find a balance between repetition that helps to reinforce the learning of vocabulary and repetition that sounds unnatural. If a pronoun is too far from its noun then the young reader's memory will be taxed. Perera (1984) recommends that repetition should not be used if it does not further the story line and only provides practice for reading aloud.

Constructing sentences

ACTIVITY 20

Sometimes specific features of sentences can cause children problems. In the following examples work out what the difficulties might be, what could cause them and how you might improve each one:

1 The opening of the letters and the reading of their contents was a simple task.

2 The opening of the letters and the reading of their contents was carried out by the postman.

3 Hannah threw the gorilla into a corner with her other toys and went back to sleep.

(*Gorilla* – Anthony Brown)

4 We stayed in all day. It was raining.

COMMENTARY

The problem with the first two is that the reader has to wait too long to get to the verb ('was' and 'was carried out'), adding considerably to the memory load. This has happened because the subject of each sentence (everything before the verb) is far too long. An additional difficulty with the second is that the verb is **passive** – a construction that children learn very late, with eight year olds still having trouble. The third raises the question of who went back to sleep. *You* know it is Hannah but the name is not repeated and 'she' is not used. When a word is missed out in this way it is called **ellipsis**, and although children can understand the construction in speech, only just over half of eight year olds are successful with written ellipsis. The fourth seems to use suitably short and simple sentences but to the young reader the relationship between them is not obvious. It is better to link them using 'because'.

Some useful rules of thumb emerge from this:

1 Get your verbs in early and prefer 'action' verbs. Avoid using the verb 'to be' too often.
2 Keep the subjects of sentences short.
3 Avoid passives.
4 Balance the need for short sentences with the need for clarity and naturalness.

Lineation

You may have noticed that the lines of text in young children's books often vary considerably in length. The position of these line breaks, a design feature called **lineation**, has an effect on the readability of the book. This section explores the relationship between lineation and readability.

ACTIVITY 21

1 Try using your intuitions about lineation.
  a In pairs suggest the position of the line breaks in the extract below.
  b Explain the principles you used to do this.
  c Suggest undesirable positions for line-breaks.

Bats make their homes in hollow trees or in buildings or caves. They hibernate together in a sheltered roost in the winter. In the summer the females hang together all day in large nursery roosts. Bats usually have only one baby each year. The baby clings to the mother while it feeds. It grows quickly and will start to fly when it is about three weeks old.

(*Animals at Home*, Dinosaur Publications, 1981)

2 The original research on lineation was carried out by Graf and Torrey in 1966. Using your knowledge of grammar if possible, explain which of these texts was easiest to read:

A

During World War 2

even fantastic schemes

received consideration

if they gave promise

of shortening the conflict.

B

During World War

2 even fantastic

schemes received

consideration if they gave

promise of shortening the
conflict.

One strategy for making a text more readable is to put the line breaks at the boundaries between the grammatical units rather than splitting them up. But the situation is a bit more complicated than that. The following text has been analysed into its clause elements with the double line showing where the line-breaks occurred. If you are unsure about **clause elements** look up the four words in the line below in the glossary.

Subject	Verb	Object	Adverbial
Most animals	make	a nest//	for their babies to be born in//
The harvest mouse	builds//	a special nest	for her babies// between the stems of plants.//

An alternative way of showing this is: SVO//A// SV//OA//A to indicate the clause elements on each line. This allows you to work out if there is a principle behind the text's lineation. For example, the above text keeps subjects and verbs together on the same line but allows an object to appear on the next line on one occasion. Adverbials can appear as complete lines. Line breaks never split up a clause element – the long adverbials, for example, are left intact.

ACTIVITY 22

Investigation
Compare two very short children's books, focusing on lineation with respect to the following questions:

1 Which clause elements are most frequently grouped together on lines?
2 Which most frequently begin/end lines?
3 Which take up whole lines in themselves?
4 Are sentences split towards the beginning or the end?
5 Are any clause elements split?
6 Is it possible to describe a consistent strategy on the part of the publisher?

You might like to compare your findings with those of various researchers:

■ It is not a good idea to end lines at sentence boundaries as this creates a line of capital letters on the left hand side.
■ If line breaks end sentences young readers tend to jump lines.
■ Line breaks should help readers to predict what is on the next line, so it is better if they occur towards the ends of sentences.

Representation

Another rich area for investigation of children's books is **representation**. This simply refers to the way in which words stand for real objects. For example, does a book use the word 'women', 'ladies' or 'girls'? This has become the territory of the political correctness movement in the last few years but the possibilities for study are not restricted to politically sensitive areas. You can look at the way children's books represent teachers, emotions, daily routines and animals, to name but a few, by examining the nouns used to label them, the way they are described, the actions they perform and so forth. This idea is explored extensively in *Children's First School Books* by Carolyn Baker and Peter Freebody.

Figure 2

ADVENTURE AT THE LIGHTHOUSE !

"THERE is going to be a bad storm tonight, Bess. I hope Grandfather is safe and snug in the lighthouse."

Tom and Bess's grand-dad was the lighthouse-keeper and they felt very worried when they saw the big black clouds blowing up.

"Let's give him a hail," suggested Bess, and they hurried to the shore, looking across the tossing waves towards the lighthouse.

"Oh, look !" cried Tom. "There's Grand-dad, and he is waving to us."

"Help !" came a voice across the water—and the children lost no time in launching their rowboat and rowing out to the distant rock.

When they reached it, poor Grand-dad sank down, clasping his foot. "I have sprained my ankle !" he gasped in dismay, as the children sprang ashore.

"And it's getting dark already !" cried Tom. "We must light the lantern."

The children assisted the old man into the lighthouse as a streak of lightning flashed across the sky and the thunder rumbled !

"Quick ! The light, Tom !" gasped Bess. "I can see a boat out there and it will surely sail on to the rocks."

The next crash of thunder seemed to shake the lighthouse, but Bess and Tom were real little children of the sea and they were not afraid.

Up the steps they raced, round and round until they reached the tower where stood the big lantern !

"I must set it going at once !" Tom panted—but as he spoke there came a tremendous flash of light, followed by a crashing of timber and broken glass.

[continued over]

Wooden beams from above tumbled down about the boy's head.

"The lightning has struck the lighthouse!" screamed Bess.

Tom had been flung to the floor, but the plucky lad scrambled up almost at once, viewing with alarm all the damage that had been done.

"The lantern is smashed!" Bess exclaimed. "Oh, Tom, what ever are we going to do now?"

For a moment brother and sister stood there in dismay, not knowing what to do. Now no friendly light could flash across the sea to warn ships away from the rocks.

But then Tom sprang to action.

"Help me bring out the wood!" he called to Bess. "We must make a warning light of some kind."

Down below on the wild sea, the folk in the sailing boat were anxiously staring into the darkness.

"Where is the lighthouse?" muttered the skipper —and as he spoke, a light flashed—a light that grew brighter and brighter at the top of the lighthouse.

Tom and Bess had made a bonfire up there from the broken wood and the rocks below were lighted up by the glare!

The little boat turned away, making for the safety of the harbour and leaving the rocks behind them.

How the children cheered as they watched.

"Well done, my dears!" cried the old lighthouse-keeper. "Those folk will always remember how you saved them."

A day or so later a mysterious box arrived at the lighthouse with a message, saying: "This is a reward for saving us from the storm."

It had been sent by the folk in the sailing vessel, and, as well as a great deal of food, the box contained a smart sailor jacket and peaked cap for Tom!

"Oh, what a wonderful gift!" exclaimed Tom. Feeling very proud, he tried on the cap and saluted smartly. "How do I look?" he asked.

"My word, lad!" said his grand-dad with a smile. "You are the smartest-looking sailor-man I have ever seen!"

ACTIVITY 23

Adventure at the Lighthouse is a short story taken from the 1956 Rainbow Annual. Examine the way in which it represents males and females. Consider the following aspects of the text:

1 The words and phrases used to describe the characters. How many references are there? What order do they occur in? What adjectives are used to describe them?
2 The actions the characters perform. What verbs are used? Can these be grouped in anyway? What adverbs are used to describe these actions?

3 What the characters say. Who speaks most? What sentence functions do they use? (Statement, exclamation, question, command.) What do they say? What speech tags are used? For example, 'said', 'exclaimed'.
4 Compare this text with a similar text published more recently.

Write an essay on the representation of gender in this text based on your findings.

Worked exam question

ACTIVITY 24

The following extract from *The Camcorder* (Oxford Reading Tree, Roderick Hunt) was used as an A-Level exam question. You are asked to 'analyse and describe' the features of language that have been used to help children's reading skills and develop their language ability.

Dad bought a camcorder.
The children had a race. Dad made a video.
"Smile everyone," said Dad.

Dad went to the sports day.
He took the camcorder.
He made a video of Wilma.

It was Jo's wedding. Dad took the camcorder.
He made a video of the wedding.

It was Mum and Dad's anniversary.
Wilma wanted to make a video.
Dad showed Wilma the camcorder.
"It's easy," he said.
Wilma made the video.
"It's easy," she said.
"Smile please!" said Wilf.

The children watched the race.
They saw the sports day.
They looked at Jo's wedding.
They laughed at Wilma's video.

They went to the tree house.
Wilma wanted to make a video.
Dad let her use the camcorder.
Wilma made the video. She saw two men.
They were burglars.
The burglars were running away.
Wilma made a video of them.
"Call the police," she shouted.
Dad got the phone. He phoned the police.
Wilma got the burglars on video.
The police came.
They looked at the video.
"Well done!" they said.
The police caught the burglars.
"Thanks to Wilma," said Dad.

COMMENTARY

■ Tends towards repetition of nouns. Only uses pronouns ('he') after extensive use of a repeated noun ('Dad'). This helps the reader to remember the characters and restricts the range of vocabulary, making the text more predictable.

■ Sentences are all simple and most of them use a subject-verb-object structure. This makes them predictable but sometimes makes the relationship between the sentences more difficult to work out and the text less like spoken language.

■ Sentences do not run onto the next line. According to many researchers this does not help young readers (see page 24).

■ The text structure uses a kind of recapping, starting 'The children watched the race'. Again this helps with predictability.

■ Speech tags ('he said' etc) only reverse the order of the usual word order (subject + verb) when the agent is a noun ('Dad') rather than a pronoun ('he'). This avoids constructions such as 'said he' which sound unnatural.

■ Nouns are not modified (as in 'the *expensive* camcorder').

■ Noun phrases are generally short. When they are longer they appear in the object position – that is, after the verb rather than before it which reflects young children's acquisition and is less of a burden on memory (e.g. 'the sports day').

■ The longer noun phrases occur together creating a predictable pattern: 'sports day' . . . 'Jo's wedding' . . . 'Wilma's video'.

■ There is a high degree of consistency of representation of sound. For almost half of the text an 'ay' sound is represented by the letter 'a', as in 'race', 'made', 'day', etc.

■ Some whole sentences are repeated some distance from each other. This develops memory whilst making reading of the repeated sentence easier.

ACTIVITY 25

Here is the complete text of *The Big Sneeze*, by Ruth Brown, for analysis. It is presented in scrambled order, each letter representing a page of the book. Unscramble the text (answer on p 29) and then consider how these features contribute to the book's purpose: vocabulary, mode, lineation, grammar, overall structure and any other features covered in this chapter.

A and panicked the terrified donkey!

B which alerted the sparrow,
who chased the spider.

C which woke the dog,
and frightened the rats –

D This wakened the cat,
who leapt at the bird –

E One hot afternoon, the farmer and
his animals were dozing in the barn. The
only sound was the buzz-buzz of the lazy fly.

F who fled from the barn,
chased by the dog –

G which scattered the startled
hens from their roost –

H "What on earth have you done? shrieked the
farmer's wife.

I This disturbed the spider,
who captured the fly –

J "ATISHOOOOOOOOOOO!" the farmer sneezed so hard
that the fly was blown up into a spider's web.

K "Nothing my dear," replied the farmer. "I only
sneezed!"

L Suddenly the buzzing stopped –
the fly had landed right on the end of the farmer's
nose.

Answers to Activity 19:
At the Seaside: page 2 – she; page 3 – the children; page 4 – they; page 5
– the children; page 6 – they. *At School*: page 1 – they; page 2 – they;
page 3 – they; page 4 – the children; page 5 – they; page 6 – they
Answers to Activity 25:
E L J I B D C F G A H K

This chapter has considered several aspects of writing for children: reading
schemes, the transition from spoken to written mode, the influence of the
oral tradition, factors that influence readability, the features of 'real books'
and representation. Missing from all of this is the business of building a
story and an indication of the kind of content that will appeal to young
children. The reading list that follows and children's books themselves will
provide plenty of sources of inspiration.

Recommended reading

Children's Books: A Parent's Guide, 1995, Puffin Books.

Children's First School Books by Carolyn Baker and Peter Freebody, 1989,
Blackwell.

Children's Reading and Writing, Katharine Perera, 1984, Blackwell.

The Identification of Readability Factors, Cliff Moon, in *The Reader and the
Text*, Edited by John Chapman, 1981, Heinemann.

The Primary English Magazine, Nov 1996, Sept 1997 etc., York Publishing
Services Ltd.

Teaching Literacy, Balancing Perspectives, Roger Beard (Ed), 1993, Hodder
and Stoughton (see especially Katharine Perera article).

3 Child-directed Speech

Even four year olds adjust their language when speaking to a two year old.
'The way that adults talk to babies is similar to the way they talk to dogs.'
(Hirsh-Pasek and Treiman, 1982)

This chapter will consider attitudes towards child-directed speech, its features and purposes, ending with a consideration of parents' monologues with pre-linguistic infants.

How do you talk to babies? It is not difficult to imagine or produce the stereotyped language used by adults to babies. Over the last twenty years interest in 'child-directed speech' – its most recent name – has grown. The topic was a late starter in terms of academic interest because earlier research suggested that babies possessed a natural device that enabled them to learn language. This led to the idea that babies learned to speak *in spite* of the poor quality input they received from their parents! The Internet question on page 31 shows how uncertain the public still are about this.

Interest sprang originally from the work of Catherine Snow in the 1970s. Since then a number of disputed questions have arisen: is child-directed speech essential for language development? How exactly does it help? Is it useful in some respects (grammatically) but detrimental in others (vocabulary)?

A big advantage of this topic is that parents are often easier to work with than children. Recording and transcribing children can be plagued with problems. But you are far more likely to get the cooperation of parents who will often chatter away using babytalk with few inhibitions.

ACTIVITY 26

Consider the implications of each of the terms (in the box below) given by researchers to child-directed speech. List the terms down the centre of a page. On one side write down the advantages of each term, on the other the disadvantages. For example, the meaning of 'babytalk' is rather unclear (does it refer to babies' language or adults'?) and is perhaps too informal for serious scientific enquiry, but its familiarity and reader friendliness would be useful in texts aimed at parents.

> motherese – parentese – caretaker language – caregiver language –
> input language – child-directed speech.

Attitudes to babytalk

'Babytalk' is the term preferred here because we are considering popular anxieties about parents using babytalk with their babies. Before considering in more detail the features of babytalk, it is worth considering two media comments in response to questions about babytalk.

ACTIVITY 27

A website you will find useful is: ask-ling@linguistlist.org. Here people ask a panel of experts about a wide range of linguistic matters. A recent question was:

'Do you have any information on the advisability, for or against, of using 'baby talk' when speaking to an infant/young toddler? Does it result in more 'advanced' language development to speak to them as you would another adult, or does 'baby talk' (saying, 'night night', 'Anna ... night, night' rather than 'it is time to go to bed now') have a purpose in language development?'

(Marcia Lewis on *Ask a Linguist*)

■ Turn the following article into a piece of advice in the style of an e-mail message in response to the above question. You may wish to supplement your answer with research using the Internet. Try searching using 'baby talk' or 'children's language'.

Baby talk important tool for learning, study says

August 1st 1997

By Lauran Neergaard

Associated Press

WASHINGTON– All that baby talk adults use with infants isn't just silly cooing. Scientists say it appears to be vital in helping babies' brains absorb key building blocks of language.

And parents do it everywhere, goo-goo-ga-gaing in English, Swedish or Russian.

University of Washington neuroscientist Patricia Kuhl says parents unconsciously exaggerate the vowel sounds that every infant – no matter what the language he or she will ultimately speak – needs to master the phonetic elements of speech.

Take the word 'bead'. People can say it so quickly that you might mistake the word for 'bed' or 'bid'. But mothers say to their babies 'Look at mommy's pretty beeeeds'.

In a study being published today in the journal *Science*, Kuhl reports that 5-month-olds begin to enunciate the three vowel sounds common to all human languages – 'ee', 'ah' and 'oo' – which are the same vowels that mothers universally stress to their babies.

This so-called parentese is 'a real tutorial on language,' Kuhl said.

At issue are infants younger than 6 months learning their first words.

Kuhl discovered in 1992 that 6-month olds learn to categorize vowel sounds that are meaningful in their native languages. She then found that they turn toward adults who speak in singsong baby talk and often ignore regular conversation. But were the actual sounds important?

Kuhl and colleagues in Sweden and Russia tape-recorded 30 women speaking to their babies. The languages were chosen because they have different vowel systems.

Whether it was Seattle moms stressing those beads or mothers in St Petersburg, Russia, admiring *bussi* – Russian for beads – they universally exaggerated the important vowels, Kuhl reports.

Such a universal effect astounded Kuhl.

'When the biology of people produces this effect so consistently across three cultures ... that tells you something,' Kuhl said. 'If you take the time to talk to your infants, biology has structured us that we know what to do.'

(Copyright *Detroit Free Press*)

■ Below is a real answer to the Internet question posed above:

I have been reading through the responses you've already gotten from this panel, and I've decided to add my voice to the lot because I saw that the opinion is pretty much split down the middle. My own position is that whether you use babytalk or not (or what form of babytalk you use) does not matter at all to your child's language development; I'll also try to explain the source for the difference in opinion among linguists.

One of the most amazing things about language is the way that children learn it in the first few years of their life. By the time children reach 3–5 years of age they have mastered most of what is complicated to learn about a language – no matter what language it is they were exposed to (or even how many languages they were exposed to!). This is really pretty amazing, given the incredible differences that exist among the world's languages.

Over the past few decades a number of anthropologists have gone to other countries to study how children acquire languages that are very different from European languages, and they have found a very striking diversity in the ways that caregivers (usually mothers, but the role of male and female siblings is often very important) talk to infants.

In some cultures, as in mainstream American, infants are treated as 'special', and elaborate vocabularies and styles of speech are developed for use when speaking to babies.

In other cultures, though, the opposite has been found to be the case: babies are expected to blend in with adult interaction (and conversation) just as soon as possible, and no special accommodation is made in speech addressed to them. And, not surprisingly, there are lots of cultures that fall in between these two polar opposites.

Again, the most interesting conclusion from this evidence – for me – is that overall all these kids learn whatever language they are learning, with whatever kind of 'input' they receive, in the same amount of time and to the same degree of competence. So, no it doesn't seem to matter how you speak to your child, as long as someone does speak to him/her.

Expert opinions differ on this issue in part because linguists have tended to study acquisition in Western countries, while anthropologists have studied acquisition of non-Western languages.

(Daniel Lefkowitz)

ACTIVITY 28

1 Compare the arguments of the original article and the Internet answer. Discuss their respective claims and how the form (newspaper report/E-mail message) of each text reflects those claims.
2 Use the same two texts to create a leaflet for parents on the advisability of using 'babytalk'. Your style should be non-technical, authoritative and not too informal. You should aim to advise and inform. Your readers are caregivers of either gender and you should assume a wide range of lifestyles and attitudes.

Vocabulary

ACTIVITY 29

1 For this activity you will be analysing the vocabulary of child-directed speech. With a partner consider these aspects of the sample:
  a The **semantic fields** (words that are related in meaning such as 'sheep' and 'cow') covered by these words; group the words into their semantic fields and write notes explaining how many there are of each. Make connections between the groups of words and the baby's world, for example, 'beddy-bye' refers to part of the baby's daily routine.
  b The sounds of the babytalk words. Categorise the words that have something in common, for example, 'brek-brek' and 'bow-wow'.
  c The connection between the babytalk and the concept it stands for, eg 'ABCs' is a part of the alphabet.

ABCs	*the alphabet*	mmmh	*appreciation of taste*
allgone	*empty, gone*	meanie	*mean person*
beddy-bye	*bed time*	nana	*grandmother*
birdie	*bird*	night-night	*goodnight*
bow-wow	*dog*	peekaboo	*game involving covering and*
buggie	*pushchair*		*uncovering eyes*
bunny	*rabbit*	pee-pee	*to urinate*
caca	*faeces*	poo	*faeces*
choo-choo	*train*	poopy	*soiled*
dada	*father*	potty	*child's pot/toilet*
din-din	*dinner*	quack-quack	*duck*
ding-dong	*penis*	tick-tock	*clock*
doggie	*dog*	tinkle	*urinate*
dolly	*doll*	tummy	*stomach*
footsie	*foot*	uh-oh	*realisation that something is wrong*
go bye-bies	*go to sleep*	upsie-daisy	*child is moving upwards*
icky	*dirty*	wee-wee	*urine/urinate*
jim-jams	*pyjamas*	winkle	*penis*
kiss it better	*consoling*	yuckie	*dirty*
mama	*mother*	yum-yum	*tasty*

2 Many of these words have become the kind of language associated with children or their carers. An important question is the extent to which they are actually used. Develop an investigation in which you look at one or more of the following:

a Which of these words carers actually claim to use. Develop a tally chart, perhaps using the above list. This could be followed up with a questionnaire on their attitudes towards babytalk – is it advisable to use it? – does it hinder language development? etc.

b Actual usage of babytalk by babies and their carers. This could be done by means of naturalistic observation – record a conversation or role play between parent and child over an extended period. But be warned! This is the most difficult way of investigating this area and you must seek permission. Don't be surprised if there are few examples of what you are looking for.

c An easier and more reliable method is to set up a simple experiment. For example, you could create a set of cards with pictures of objects and then ask a young child to name the objects. How will you deal with actions or exclamations?

Features and purposes

ACTIVITY 30

Child-directed speech aims to:

1 attract and hold the baby's attention;
2 help the process of breaking down language into understandable chunks;
3 make the conversation more predictable by keeping the conversation in the 'here and now' and referring to things that the baby can see.

■ With a partner, rate the extent to which each of the features below might help to achieve the above aims. So, if you think that **A** helps to attract attention and make conversation predictable, write **1** and **3** alongside **A**.

A Higher pitch and exaggerated **intonation and stress**.

B Repeated **sentence frames**. This occurs when the parent uses the same structure over and over, filling in part of it with a different word each time, eg 'That's a —'.

C Repetition and partial repetition of the adult's own words.

D Questions and commands (getting the child to do something).

E Frequent use of the child's name and an absence of pronouns (However, Durkin (1995) disputes this – see recommended reading on page 87).

F Absence of past tenses (eg threw, ran, played).

G A large number of one word utterances.

H Use of simple sentences (eg Shoogle is a nice cat; Fred eats rats).

I Omission of **inflections** such as plurals (plane<u>ts</u>) and possessives (mummy'<u>s</u>).

J Fewer verbs, **modifiers** (adjectives in front of nouns) and function words (such as 'at' 'my' – see page 44).

K Use of **concrete nouns** (cat, train) and dynamic verbs (give, put).

L Use of **expansions** – where the adult fills out the child's utterance.

M Use of **re-castings** – where the baby's vocabulary is put into a new utterance.

ACTIVITY 31

The following transcript is of an 18 month old baby, Katharine, and her mother.

1 Find as many of the above features of child-directed speech as you can.

2 Do you think the mother's language appears to assist the baby? (If you have the tape, consider the effect of intonation).

3 Write up the analysis as a short essay.

4 Compare the mother's language with that of the other transcripts in this book.

Tape Extract 2

1 K:　I stuck.

2 M:　You're stuck. There. Is that better?

3 K:　Yeh.

4 M:　You alright now?

5 K:　Got my socks on.

6 M:　You have. What colour are your socks?

7 K:　Pink.

8 M:　Yes, they are pink.

9 K:　[*indeciph*] put my slippers on.

10 M:　Mmm. What colour are your slippers?

11 K:　Um. Red.

12 M:　Red. Red and . . .

13 K:　O . . . don't know . . . and . . .

14 M:　And . . . (2) red and . . . what?

15 K:　Red and blue.

16 M:　Red and blue. Yes, they are. They're red and blue slippers.

17 K:　With zip.

18 M:　With a zip.

COMMENTARY The transcript in Activity 31 contains several features of child-directed speech. In utterance **2** the mother's first sentence can be regarded as an expansion. In utterance **6** 'colour' is stressed and the mother repeats the word 'sock' in a new sentence – an example of re-casting as well as avoidance of the pronoun 'they' that might have replaced 'socks' in adult conversation. Utterance **8**, as well as confirming that the child is correct, is also an expansion. In the next utterance the child takes the initiative and the adult takes the opportunity to re-cast and repeat 'slippers', whilst also repeating the frame, 'What colour are . . .?' In utterances **12** and **14** the adult uses 'and' as a prompt, providing a slot for the baby to fill and suggesting that the baby does know the answer. Utterance **16** is an expansion into a full sentence, incorporating repetition of the key vocabulary of the last few utterances. Utterance **18** is an expansion.

In the first half of the transcription there are a large number of questions from the mother and, in the second half, the prompts act as directives for the child to provide the name of the second colour. There doesn't seem to be an active avoidance of pronouns ('you', 'your', 'they') but here the mother is probably taking her cue from the baby who does not refer to herself using her first name but uses the pronoun 'I'. Elsewhere, the use of pronouns is carefully measured against repetition: 'socks' is repeated in **6** before being replaced by 'they' in **8**; in line **16** 'they' is initially used to replace the earlier 'slippers' but as this occurred six utterances earlier it is soon repeated in order to reduce the memory load on the child. Finally, utterance **16** shows an interesting example of partial repetition. The first 'red and blue' is a simple repetition confirming that the answer is finally right. 'Yes, they are' again confirms the answer but it also provides the subject ('they') and verb ('are') of the full sentence that is to follow. The adult has broken the sentence down into its constituents before uttering it in full.

ACTIVITY 32

Katharine (K), aged 18 months, and her mother (M) are playing with a train set. The transcript below is missing most of the mother's contributions. They are marked with a horizontal line.

1 Using as much information as possible about child-directed speech write the adult's contributions to this conversation.
2 If you have the cassette tape try this follow-up activity:
  a Transcribe the mother's actual contribution to the conversation.

b Analyse this contribution for features of child-directed speech. Don't forget that you will also be able to find examples of feature A – higher pitch and exaggerated intonation.
c Compare your version with the original in terms of child-directed speech.
3 You can have additional practice at identifying these features by listening to **Tape Extract 6** which is transcribed on page 85 in chapter 7.

Tape Extract 3

1	K:	These are mine.
2	M:	Yes, it's a big bridge, isn't it. Is the train going under the bridge?
3	K:	Can't!
4	M:	_____

5 K: Can't, can't, can't.

6 M: It's because the tractor's in the way. (4) [*K wheels the train*]

7 K: Bye people! Bye people!

8 M: Here they come again (1) Here come the people (1) on the train.

9 K: [*indecipherable*]

10 M: _____

11 K: Daddy

12 M: _____

13 K: And Grandma

14 M: _____

15 K: And Craig

16 M: Yes

17 K: Uh and Pamela

18 M: _____

19 K: That one.

20 M: _____

21 K: Bye very... bye people! (1) There's a cow.

22 M: _____

23 K: Dink of water

24 M: _____

25 K: Yeh. Having orange.

26 M: _____

27 K: Wat...

28 M: _____

29 K: No

30 M: No, they drink water [*M now changes topic*] _____

31 K: Eddie

32 M: _____

33 K: Driving cactor [*tractor*]

34 M: Where's Katharine?

35 K: Um (1) In there. In there. [*points to cabin of train*]

36 M: _____

37 K: She's in there.

38 M: _____

39 K: She got her body.

40 M: _____Is she driving the train?

41 K: Yeh

42	M:	_____
43	K:	Got her back.
44	M:	Her back? Where's her back?
45	K:	In front. (1)
46	M:	_____ [*mystified*]
47	K:	Bye dinner! bye dinner! bye dinner!
48	M:	_____
49	K:	He's having [*unclear*] drink. You do it.
50	M:	OK

ACTIVITY 33

1 Write a short piece of advertising blurb for a cassette that claims to teach parents how to talk to children.
2 Find a wordless picture book or a picture book with words covered or deleted (eg *Clown* by Quentin Blake). Ask an adult to re-tell the story for a young child of about five years and record it. There are then some alternative ways of continuing. You could keep the adult talking, perhaps asking them about the story they have just told, or you could ask another adult to tell you the story in the pictures. Either way, compare the language of the adult when pretending to address a child with addressing yourself.

Does child-directed speech influence children's language development?

It is one thing to show that adults talk to babies in a special way but it is a lot more difficult to demonstrate that such talk helps language development. Certainly, it is common sense that child-directed speech should help babies to learn. But does it?

In some obvious ways it does seem to help. Children tend to imitate the stressed words in a sentence so when adults use exaggerated intonation patterns they help children to find these words. Adults tend to label objects at an intermediate level of generality, calling tulips, roses and bluebells 'flowers' because this is the level at which the baby is likely to respond to these items. That is, babies don't care about different types of flowers – they are likely to destroy any kind they come across!

Parents use questions where the W-word doesn't appear in its usual place but where the baby must replace with a word, as in:
Child: I ate it
Mother: You ate what? (rather than 'What ...?')
Child: The candy

The research literature is full of examples like these. But is it possible to show that child-directed speech actually improves a child's acquisition of language? This sounds like a simple enough question to answer. Surely if you can show that parents who use a lot of child-directed speech have children who are advanced linguistically then you have proved your point. But, in fact it's not that simple. And then if you do find some connection between the two what exactly has caused one to influence the other?

For many years this question caused a great deal of disagreement. Some researchers found that child-directed speech was very important, even essential for language learning. Others felt that it only played a marginal role, not influencing children's language to any great extent. Some specific findings were:

- a parent's use of questions with 'yes' / 'no' answers seems to be connected with many aspects of children's language development;
- complexity in a parent's language hinders language development;
- a very persistent finding has been that the use of child-directed speech improves the child's use of auxiliary verbs such as 'could', 'have', 'did', 'might'.

There is a popular belief that babies learn language because adults correct them when they go wrong. To some extent this is true but the process is by no means as straightforward as many would believe. A great deal depends on which aspect of language is being corrected. For example, there are many examples of how not to attempt correcting pronunciation as in the well-known 'fis phenomenon'. Here a child persistently says 'fis' instead of 'fish', but when an adult says 'fis' the child complains that it should be 'fish', unaware that he/she is still saying 'fis'! However, indirect grammatical correction as in expansions and re-castings (see p 34) can be of benefit. Experiments have also shown that over-correction can have a detrimental effect on a baby: imagine what you would feel like if those around you responded primarily to the correctness of your language and were less interested in what you had to say. You would probably end up afraid to say anything for fear that you had made a mistake.

Experiments designed to give babies a greater experience of expansions did not have any effect on their language learning. The richness and variety of language spoken to babies may have more effect than the number of expansions used. This was confirmed in a piece of research by Keith Nelson who had adults not only expand but also re-cast their babies' sentences, as in: 'Doggy eat' which became 'What is the doggy eating?' in the adult's reply.

Children who had experienced this, later performed much better on imitation tests. However, in normal conversation re-castings such as these are not very common in the speech of parents to their children and so they may not play a very important part in development. When they are used they may serve to draw the baby's attention to their own language and thereby help to improve performance.

An interesting recent development in this issue is the possibility that child-directed speech does not directly help babies to learn language. Instead it may help parents and baby to communicate, it may help the parent with expression of feelings or even help the parent to control the baby. In other words its purpose may be primarily social rather than educational.

The debate about child-directed speech continues. But there are a few facts. Some non-Western cultures don't use child-directed speech at all so it clearly isn't essential for language learning. One theory is that Western society is very child-centred and so adults go a long way towards meeting the needs of the child. Other cultures emphasise the child's need to learn about the language of particular situations so they compromise far less for the sake of the child and so don't use child-directed speech.

Parents' pre-linguistic monologues

Most of the research into child-directed speech has looked at parents speaking with babies who can already use some words. But in fact parents use child-directed speech before babies can make any verbal contribution to the 'conversation'. Such language is therefore effectively a monologue on the part of the parent. One interesting question for research in this area has been to examine parents' styles in using this talk to see if it makes any difference to the baby's ultimate development.

ACTIVITY 34

Here are two extracts from parents' monologues with pre-linguistic babies. The mothers were asked to get the baby's attention and play with him/her as they normally did. Both babies, the first a boy, the second a girl, are aged six weeks.

How would you characterise the differences between the two monologues? Consider the purposes of each utterance and the assumptions made by the mothers.

Monologue 1
Come on.
Talk.
Talk to me.
Can you talk to me?
[*laugh*] Say something.
Come on.
Talk.
Can you talk?
Can you say something?
Well, talk.
Well, say something.
Can you say Mama?
Well, come on.
Come on.
Come on.
Come on.

Monologue 2
Is that a burp?
Huh?
Or are you going to get the hiccups?
You going to get the hiccups?
Huh?
Yeah.
Hi, there.
You look like you're just concentrating so hard.
Roseann.
Hello.
What?
What?
Hey, you follow me, don't you?
You follow my voice.
You follow my voice more than you follow me.
Yes.

(Kenneth Kaye, Methuen, 1984, p 198)

COMMENTARY   In Monologue 1 the mother repeats imperatives (commands) and requests. In Monologue 2 there is more variety and the mother assumes that the baby is already making a meaningful contribution, allowing these to direct her own utterances. Recent research has shown that pre-linguistic babies make an enormous contribution to 'conversations' in this way and that parents who are more responsive have a significant effect on their baby's rate of linguistic development (see chapter 6). In particular, this is true of parents who make specific references (they say 'chair' and not 'furniture' or 'that') to objects that the baby is currently attending to. It is the precise manner in which this reference is made rather than the kind of word used ('choo choo' for train) that is important. In spite of some of the claims on previous pages for the benefits of child-directed language, the effect on grammar is regarded as very slight, although there are some positive effects on the baby's vocabulary. In chapter 7 we will follow up the theoretical implications of these findings.

ACTIVITY 35

Apply the ideas arising from the foregoing comments to the following transcription of a mother's monologue spoken whilst changing her 10 week old son's nappy. You may also wish to look for features from elsewhere in this chapter and anything else you have learned about child-directed speech.

Mother: Soaked to the skin, aren't you. Soaked to the skin. Yeh! Yeh! Aren't you soaked to the skin. Yeh. Ooh! Smell that fart. Ughh! Dirty Mummy. Dirty Mummy. Now, where the devil … Ooh! Big stretch! Are you going to sleep a long time again like you did last night? I bet you won't. It's unlikely you'll do … I was most impressed by your sleeping last night, darling [*indecipherable*] Weren't you a good boy. I woke up and I thought oh, probably only about eleven o'clock and I haven't heard Daddy come home. And I put the light on and I thought 'Blimey! You're asleep!' Asleep all that time. I couldn't believe it. No! I couldn't believe it. It was a big surprise. Yeh. A big surprise. [*Baby makes noises*] A very big surprise [*indecipherable*] Yeh. Are you going to put this on, eh? Are you going to put this on? Are we? Yeh! That's a big smile [*indecipherable*]. There we are. Right, put your head in here. Are you going to put your head in there? Are we? Yeh!

ACTIVITY 36

Here are some ideas for further investigations into child-directed speech (CDS):

1 Compare the speech of a mother or father to a young baby (about two) with their speech to a ten year old.
2 Compare a parent's pretended CDS with the real thing when the child is present.
3 Do non-parents show an ability to use CDS compared with real parents?

4 Compare the language of a pre-linguistic monologue with caregiver language involving a speaking baby.
5 Does CDS avoid pronouns? Durkin gives examples such as, 'I think Mummy might have to blow hers.' – which contains two pronouns and a noun referring to the same person.
6 Compare mothers' and fathers' CDS.

This chapter has focused on the language of adults interacting with their babies. There is currently a great deal of interest in this area of research. The popular view that 'baby talk' is harmful is being replaced by exaggerated claims for its benefits. However, it has proved difficult to show how or why child-directed speech is beneficial for children. Some highly specific advantages have been found, such as when parents use yes/no questions or refer to objects that the child is currently focusing on. However, it is possible that child-directed speech aids parent/baby communication and not language learning directly. Finally, some cultures do not use child-directed speech so it cannot be essential for first language learning.

Recommended reading

Speaking with Style, Elaine Slosberg Andersen, 1990, Routledge.

Language Experience and Early Language Development, Margaret Harris, 1992, Lawrence Erlbaum Associates (an advanced text).

Learning to Be Literate, Alison Garton and Chris Pratt, 1998, Blackwell.

4 Fitting Words Together – The Beginnings of Grammar

'A sentence is a big word with holes in it'

(a five year old)

This chapter takes you from when children first put words together up to the point at about the age of four or five when most of the grammatical rules of English have been conquered. Although grammar is the main focus here and usually provides the basis for stage theories (see p 3), this chapter will also include pragmatic development. Chapter 5 concentrates on vocabulary and phonology.

The two word stage

At around 18 months of age babies begin to combine words to form two word utterances. Why do they do this? Possible answers are that the baby hears several words at a time in the language going on around her. She may also start to realise that two words produce clearer meanings than one. Whatever the reason behind this development, it marks a breakthrough – the beginnings of grammar. Before looking at the work of researchers in this area, work through the activities below.

ACTIVITY 37

How do you know when two words are really being combined? Take the words 'look' and 'here'. Experiment with ways of saying them together in that order. Consider the contexts in which they would be used. Which combinations would you regard as genuine two word combinations and which not?

ACTIVITY 38

1 Working with one other person, attempt to hold a conversation using only two words at a time before giving the other person a turn. Either record the conversation or write down as many of the combinations used as you can after you have finished. You will find it useful to decide on a topic of conversation before you start.

2 Now try the same conversation using full adult utterances, then discuss:
  a how the words in the two word conversation were chosen (compared with the full utterances);
  b the order of the words in the two word utterances; and
  c difficulties in getting yourself understood.

English has evolved as a language for which word order is crucially important. The young baby has to learn how word order and objects in the environment are connected. Imagine a language with words like 'lakarmey' and 'timreph'. You are approached by a member of a culture completely unknown to you. She says: 'lakarmey timreph'. Later you hear 'timreph lakarmey'. You would assume that the two utterances mean different things. In the same way, word order was important in getting yourself understood in the two word conversation you had above.

ACTIVITY 39

1 To what extent do you agree that the two word stage creates meaning through words only? Discuss this with a partner.
2 What do you think the baby is trying to say in the following extract? The solution is at the end of the chapter.

Baby: Daddy, daddy king, daddy king (0.5), k . . . k . . . daddy king.

Father: Daddy king?

Baby: Daddy shing, ching, daddy k . . . key . . . king.

Father: I like kings? He's got a beard, so he might . . . might be a king. I don't know but he's certainly wearing very funny clothes.

Baby: Daddy king, daddy king, daddy king.
          (Jean Aitchison, *Reith Lecture*, 1996)

ACTIVITY 40

The following table shows typical examples of two word utterances spoken by babies. Below it are two grammars that have been used to 'explain' the utterances.

baby bed	baby like	dolly there	baby cry
there teddy	mummy drink	where mummy	comb hair
baby table	gone milk	toy gone	daddy pen
mummy gone	mummy car	my doggie	milk cup
silly hat	she silly	funny pussy	

1 Here are two possible ways of explaining these combinations. Apply them to the data and decide which one best explains it.

a

a person performs an action

a person or object is described

an action affects an object

an object is located

an object is given a possessor

(based on Crystal, 1986)

b

Pivot grammar (Braine, 1963). Pivot words appear repeatedly and are always in the same position. 'Open' words appear last.

2 As an extension activity, try applying 'adult' clause elements (subject, verb, object, adverbial etc) to the two word utterances. Call this theory **2** and match your findings against the categories of theory **1a**. It will help if you put the missing words into the two word utterances. Which is the most useful – theory **1a** or **2**?

COMMENTARY   You should have found that theory **1a** explains the purposes (or the semantic relations) of most of the utterances. Theory **1b** explains some of the ways in which the words are combined but has largely been discredited as a description of a two word grammar. For theory **1a** you may have found that noun plus noun combinations were the most difficult to categorise as they can have more than one semantic relationship – a person performs an action or an object is given a possessor.

Telegraphic speech

Many researchers regard this as the next stage after the two word stage, although some experts also apply the term 'telegraphic' to the two word stage. 'Telegraphic' is meant to reflect the character of telegrams which were once the only way of conveying information quickly across huge distances. The idea was to keep the message short in order to keep costs minimal, as in: *'Mother ill/will go immediately/stay home'*. During approximately the third year children will produce language something like a telegram; for example, *'I show book'; 'I very tall'; 'That car?'* That is, they will tend to retain **content words** (usually nouns, verbs, and adjectives that refer to real things) and drop **function words** (that have a grammatical function, such as pronouns, prepositions, auxiliary verbs). The former also usually include inflections – changes to words such as -s for plurals and -ed endings for past tense – although these are not complete words in themselves. As with all stages, the child's language does not stay still but slowly approximates more and more to adult speech. There is therefore a gradual increase in the baby's MLU as function words and inflections are added.

ACTIVITY 41

The following data was collected by giving children a model sentence to copy – see the left-hand column. The responses are from different children at different ages.

Model	25 months	28 months	35 months
I showed you the book	I show book	I show book	show you the book
I am very tall	My tall	I very tall	I very tall
I do not want an apple	I do apple	I do a apple	I don't want apple
I am drawing a dog	drawing dog	I draw dog	I am drawing a dog
I will read the book	read book	I will read book	I will read the book

(adapted from Brown and Fraser, 1963 (in Brown/Lee p 168))

1 Which word classes (nouns, verbs, etc) are most frequently imitated in the above data?
2 What changes take place with age?
3 Brown and Fraser found the following percentages of correctly imitated words in various classes. Compare these findings against the above data.

inflections (*-ed, -s*)	44%	'to be'	33%
pronouns (*us, you*)	72%	nouns	·100%
articles (*a/the*)	39%	main verbs	85%
modal auxiliary (*can, might*)	56%	adjectives	92%

4 Collect your own data, trying out one or two of the following variations:
  a using the imitation method;
  b using naturalistic data and compare which words are omitted in the imitation method;

  c testing the hypothesis that telegraphic utterances preserve the word order of adult English.

Pronouns

The advantage with pronouns (*I, me, this, that,* etc) is that you don't have to keep repeating the name of the person you are talking to. Adults sometimes compensate for children's lack of skill with pronouns by using names (or roles) excessively when talking to children, so that it is not uncommon to hear requests like: *Julie come and play?* But why might children find pronouns difficult?

The obvious problem is that pronouns change their meaning depending on the context in which they are used, so that *me* can refer to *Daddy, Mummy* or whoever is speaking, but the speaker can also refer to *you* who can be just about anyone else in the room. The complications multiply when there are more people present and *he* and *we* are introduced.

ACTIVITY 42

1 Researchers have yet to agree on an order in which pronouns are learned and there may be considerable variation from person to person. Using the following list and the researchers' suggestions below, discuss with someone else what you think the order of acquisition might be.

> **subject** pronouns: *I, you, he, she, it, we, you* (plural), *they*
> **object** pronouns: *me, him, her, us, them*
> **demonstrative** pronouns: *this, that*

- One of the parents is frequently absent during the day and is therefore likely to be talked about.
- Children learn pronouns that stand for things they have already named. These tend to be things in the immediate here and now.
- Children frequently omit the subject from their early sentences (as in '*Don't want to*').

2 Analyse Katharine's use of pronouns in the transcript on page 52: **Tape extract 5**.
3 Show a child of about 3 to 5 years old a picture. Describe it using pronouns, for example, *The boy told his mother a funny story and she laughed.* Then ask the child to talk about the picture themself. Does the child use the pronouns or replace them with nouns and noun phrases?
  (based on Thieman, 1974, in Perera, p 104)

COMMENTARY The earliest pronouns to appear are usually the ones that refer to things –
it, *this* and *that*. Personal pronouns begin in the third year but confusions
will continue for some time, for example between *I* and *me*. The latter are
usually used before third person (*he/she*) which come before the second
person (*you*). Singular forms are learned before plurals.

Making words

One of the most interesting things about children's language is that it is
creative in ways that adults often find entertaining. This sometimes
involves 'mistakes'. **Over-generalisation** occurs when children have learned
a rule and they apply it inappropriately. For example, the -ed **bound
morpheme** that creates the past tense is often applied to create forms such
as *goed*. For Roger Brown, the use of such bound morphemes (that cannot
stand on their own) marks the move from Stage 1 to Stage 2 grammar at
about the age of two years (see page 3).

ACTIVITY 43

The following transcription illustrates this
process. Discuss how the examples of over-
generalisation it contains differ in construction.

(This transcript appears some way into **Tape
Extract 5** of the cassette).

> **M**: What was he doing in the garden?
>
> **K**: He had the noisy tractor.
>
> **M**: Did he? Was he riding it or driving it?
>
> **K**: Driving it.
>
> **M**: Driving it.
>
> **K**: He went the funny way.
>
> **M**: Did he?
>
> **K**: Yeh. He satted on the truck.
>
> **M**: He sat on the truck, did he? Then what did he do?
>
> **K**: Drived the seat.
>
> **M**: He drove the seat, did he?
>
> **K**: Yeh.

- The earliest verbs to have -ed morphemes are those which describe complete actions that can be easily perceived by children (eg *opened*).
- These can be contrasted with verbs describing continuous activities with less clear cut endings (eg *talked*). These are less easily learned by children.
- The linguistic complexity of the verb itself is also an important factor. A child may be thinking about 'pastness' and therefore works out that an '-ed' ending is required. But does the child also need to think about singular and plural? For some verbs this is clearly not an issue, as in: *I opened* versus *they opened*, whereas for others such as *I was* versus *we were* there is this additional problem.

ACTIVITY 44

1 Which past tense forms are easier to learn? Put the following verbs into the likely order of learning using the above principles (many of them will tie for position). It may be useful to write out the past tense forms for each one using the format: *I, you, s/he(it), we, you* (plural), *they*.
to push   to be   to open   to go   to walk   to see

2 Explain why you think the present participle ending -ing is learned before the past tense marker -ed.

3 Why do younger children sometimes get -ed endings right before they start getting them wrong?

4 Do you think that the frequency with which words are spoken to children is an important factor in learning to use morphemes? Compare the two lists below and comment on what they suggest about how children learn about such morphemes. What does this suggest about the role of imitation in language acquisition?

From the earliest to the latest learned by children

1) -ing

2) plural -s

3) possessive s

4) the, a

5) past tense -ed

6) third person singular -s

7) auxiliary be

From the most to the least frequently used by parents

the, a

-ing

plural -s

auxiliary be

possessive -s

third person singular -s

past tense -ed

(F. Katamba, *On Becoming a Speaking Mammal*, 1996, Longman)

5 Comment on K's ability to use bound morphemes in the transcript on page 52 – **Tape extract 5**.

COMMENTARY

Children usually learn the '-ing' morpheme before the '-ed' because it refers to the present time and initially children's language is strongly linked to the 'here and now'. Some parents become alarmed when their baby seems to go backwards by getting '-ed' endings right for a while and then starting to get them wrong. This happens because at first the baby is not aware that '-ed' creates the past tense, or indeed that it is a separate element added on to an existing word. Linguists say that this use of the past tense is **unanalysed**. Moving onto **4**, if children's acquisition of new morphemes was only influenced by how often they were used by the adults around them we would expect the two columns to match each other exactly. There are some similarities: for example, '-ing' and plural '-s' are used frequently by adults and are learned early by babies. But by and large the table suggests that the frequency with which an adult uses a morpheme does not influence the speed with which a child learns that particular morpheme. Bear this in mind during chapter 7 when considering theories of language acquisition.

ACTIVITY 45

Plurals can easily be investigated by creating a series of pictures showing single examples of various objects followed by several examples of the same thing. Choose your items carefully so that you test the child on both regular and irregular plurals, common and uncommon words. For example, *horse, shoe, child, sheep*. Take into account that forming one plural using '-s' might influence the child into doing the same for the following items.

ACTIVITY 46

The plurals of compound nouns make for interesting investigations. Show a 3–5 year old child a puppet or perhaps a picture of a strange animal. Tell them that he is a monster who likes to eat mud and ask them what they would call him. Then tell the child, *a mudeater*. By varying what the monster eats you can test the child's ability to form compounds. Try *mice, rats, sheep, children* etc but vary the way the word forms the plural. The original research found that even children who over-generalised *mouse* to *mouses* in their normal speech, created a *mice-eater* on this occasion. So this could be combined with Activity 45. There are several ways in which you can vary this experiment but it is very helpful to work out the adult rules for forming compounds in this way.

(Based on research by Peter Gordon)

What words do – pragmatic development

Pragmatics is the branch of linguistics that deals with what words do or achieve rather than with strictly what they mean. For example, if I say *door* you know that it refers to that thing we open when we go into rooms – a matter of semantics. But the pragmatics of *door!* are about whether I mean *Shut it!* (commanding you) or *It's about to slam* (informing you). Pragmatics also covers such issues as knowing how to ask and answer questions in a conversation.

Even before they have said anything that sounds remotely like a word babies know that utterances can work for them in a number of ways. The most famous work in this field is that of Michael Halliday who studied the functions of his son's language. For example, at nine months he used four functions, two of which were the *I want* (instrumental) and the *Do as I tell you* (regulatory) function. By one year each one of these functions could be sub-divided and by nearly two years three more functions had been added. So Halliday sees the child's range of functions as increasing over the first two years. However, Halliday's is a complex system and can be difficult to apply to data.

A simpler system is that of John Dore, shown in the table below:

Speech act	Example
Labelling	touches a doll's eyes and says *eyes*
Repeating	says what an adult has just said
Answering	answers adult's question
Requesting action	unable to push a peg through a hole says *uh uh uh* whilst looking at parent
Calling	shouts for parent across room
Greeting	shouts *hi!*
Protesting	shouts when parent attempts to put on shoe
Practising	utters word when person or object not present

(in Foster and adapted, 1990, Longman, p 63)

An important influence of work such as this is that it emphasised the social context of language – ie the child learns to do things with language because of his need to communicate with others. It was a challenge to those who believed that babies are innately pre-programmed to learn language.

ACTIVITY 47

1 Find out Halliday's functions, collect some data from a young child and apply both Halliday and Dore. Compare the effectiveness of the two systems for describing the functions of the baby's language. Consider questions such as: which system is the easier to apply and why? Can each system deal with every utterance in your data? Are there any functions in each system that are not used and why might this be the case?

2 This is a conversation between a 14 month old child and her father.
   a Decide on the purposes of the child's utterances using Dore's classification.
   b Write an entertaining piece building on what the baby might be thinking if she had full adult abilities. For example, imagine that what the adult thinks the baby intends is vastly different from the truth.

Jess: Book.
Dad: Yes, it's your book. Do you like that one?

Jess: Book.
Dad: You want me to read it?
Jess: Yes. Read.
Dad: Come and sit here then. 'Oh look, here are some horses.'
Jess: Horses.
Dad: And who is this?
Jess: Dog.
Dad: Yes a dog. A big brown dog.
Jess: Shop.
Dad: Shop?
Jess: Yea. Shop. Dog.
Dad: Oh yes, we saw Jim's dog in the shop.
Jess: Jim.
Dad: Is this like Jim's dog?
Jess: Yes.
Dad: A bit. And what's this?
Jess: Baa.
Dad: That's right – a sheep. It says baa.

(adapted from Clare Shaw, 1993, Hodder)

ACTIVITY 49

Compare your analysis of the above transcript with the functions used by Katharine (at 27 months) below. Apply Dore or Halliday or develop your own functions based on an adult model; for example, you might begin by listing all the possible adult functions, such as – persuade, advise, instruct, encourage, illustrate, etc – then apply these to the data below. The context of the conversation is a role play on fixing a car. If you have the cassette, this is Tape Extract 4.

Tape Extract 4

M: Needs a bit more. Better put some oil in. Oil's a bit heavy. We'd better do that together.

K: [*appropriate noises*]

M: 'S'right. Put it back on.

K: Put back on.

M: Everything else OK?

K: Yeh.

M: Looks fine. Battery looks fine.

K: But (?) we … we have to fix the wheels.

M: Ooh, right. What've we got to do to the wheels? We've checked the tyre pressure haven't we. Think that's right. We checked the tyre pressure with the pump, didn't we?

K: Sh'we check de pyre … tryre pe … pessure?

M: Shall we check them again?

K: Yeh.

M: Oh, right, OK. [*various 'pshshshsh' noises*]

M: Looks OK to me.

K: Looks OK to me.

M: Looks about right.

K: Looks 'bout right.

M: Okay, take it off, put the little top on.

K: Put little top on.

M: Cap on. Right. Check the other one. [*noises*]

K: And that way. And that way.

M: Oh right, OK.

K: And you're that way. You have de red pen. There's a red pen for ya.

M: Right.

K: I'm doing the tyre pressures. Pshsh. Pshsh. Pshsh. Put little lid on. Put in the fridge to cool it down.

M: [*laughs*] Put what in the fridge? What are you going to put in the fridge?

K: De oil.

Asking questions and saying 'no!'

Asking questions and saying 'no' are two things that we might expect children to do well!

This section examines in more detail how children construct these two functions of language. Ursula Bellugi suggests these stages for forming negatives (approximate ages are given in brackets):

Stage 1	Stage 2	Stage 3
(2 years)	(2 years 3 months)	(2 years 9 months)
No . . . wipe finger	I can't catch you	This can't stick
No sit there	You can't dance	I didn't did it
Where mitten no	I don't know his name	I didn't caught it
No fall!	That no fish school	Donna won't let go
Not my bed	He no bite you	That was not me
		I not crying

ACTIVITY 50

1 Convert the above utterances into the equivalent adult utterances and then create **affirmative** sentences from them. Look closely at how the negative was formed in the adult sentences and try to work out some of the rules for doing this. For example:

Affirmative
a I go to the cinema
b I went to the cinema

Negative
I do not go to the cinema
I did not go to the cinema

In these two sentences the auxiliary verb *do* is added in the same tense as the main verb in the affirmative sentence (ie present in **a** and then past in **b**). *Not* is then placed immediately after the auxiliary in both cases.

2 Now work out the baby's rules for forming the negative at each stage. Consider word order and variation in the words that help to create the negative.

COMMENTARY

At Stage One the baby produces affirmative sentences with *no* added to the beginning or the end. This is the only way of producing negatives. At Stage Two there is more variety of method with *can't* and *don't* being used but without variation of tense. It is unlikely that there is any sense of this being *can* + *not* since children tend to learn *can't* and *don't* before *can* and *do*. *No* is also retained but it now appears in mid-utterance in what will eventually be the appropriate position for *not* when it emerges – that is before the main verb. At Stage Three there is more variety in the tense of the auxiliary verb which now seems to be used appropriately. In *That was not me*, 'not' is moved to a position after the main verb, another feature of the rule in operation. At this final stage much has been achieved but, as you can see, there are still some issues to be resolved.

ACTIVITY 51

Investigate a child's ability to form negatives. Introduce the child to two puppets who never agree with each other. So if one of them says, *My ball is red*, the other says, *Your ball isn't red*. After a few demonstrations ask the child to work one of the puppets. Vary the kinds of sentences used to explore the ways in which the child forms negatives. It is also important that the sentences make sense to the child.

Asking questions

Children begin to ask questions during the second year. There is some agreement about the ways in which they form questions at various ages. The following activity will help you to work them out.

ACTIVITY 52

1 Turn the following statements into questions:
   a as an adult would;
   b as a child would using the number of words shown in brackets.

For example, *Mummy is here* (2) would become a *Is Mummy here?* And b *Mummy here?*

Daddy is coming home (2)
This is something (1)

That is something (2 or 1)
It has gone somewhere (3)
I saw that (4)
You can help me (4)
We can sleep somewhere (4)

2 Compare the adult and the child versions. Explain how they each form questions.
3 Suggest some stages that children might go through in constructing questions.

COMMENTARY

Here are some possible ways that a child could produce questions from the above: *Daddy come; whatisdis; what that; where it gone; did I saw that; can you help me; where we can sleep.* Three stages are involved: at first rising intonation but no grammar is used; then the baby grasps wh- words such as *when, where, what,* etc; then she learns to turn round the auxiliary verb (*can*) and the subject of the sentence (*You*).

ACTIVITY 53

Carry out a full analysis of the following data using the ideas studied in this chapter. The transcript is a conversation between Katharine at 27 months and her mother. Consider these aspects of the baby's speech: ability to use verbs (tenses, tag questions); functions and conversational (pragmatic) skills;

use of inflections; the MLU, comparing the score with Brown's stages (see page 3); negatives; questions. Approach the text systematically by underlining the features you are interested in and making notes. Then write an essay explaining the way in which Katharine uses these features in the context.

Tape Extract 5

Key: the transcript has been simplified. Only longer pauses have been shown, eg (3). Otherwise conventional punctuation has been used. **K**: the baby, Katharine. **M**: mother.

1 K: What did you say? (2)

2 M: Didn't say anything (2) What do you want to do? (2)

3 K: Does it open?

4 M: Er yes.

5 K: Oh, ah, aaaahhhh! I o …, I uh … I want to do that, didn't I.

6 M: What did you do? What did you do, Katharine? Did you open it?

7 K: Yeh. Took this out. Me took this out. This one out. Look, look what, look what it's got on its front.

8 M: What has it got?

9 K: It's got lady with those long things on. That's a bit funny.

10 M: Mmm. What else has it got?

11 K: What's those . . .? What're they? What're they? What're they, Mummy?

12 M: What're what?

13 K: Those bottles.

14 M: Show me.

15 K: There.

16 M: Um. It's just a picture of some bottles. I'm not sure what's in there.

17 K: What's in there?

18 M: I'm not sure. What do you think?

19 K: I d'know. (3)

20 M: Shall we put it back?

21 K: No (5) I want to do some of that, please. (4) Can I have a piece of paper please?

22 M: No.

23 K: Thank you.

24 M: What are you going to do?

25 K: I'm going to draw a picture of somebody, okay.

26 M: Mm huh.

27 K: Somebody who's black.

28 M: Okay.

29 K: Who's called Jesse.

30 M: Oh I see.

31 K: We haven't got pi . . . black today, have we.

32 M: No, that's red. Do you want me to get you a black?

33 K: Yes please.

ACTIVITY 54

The cassette tape extends the above transcript for several minutes. Transcribe it using a suitable and consistent transcription code. For example: you may or may not use conventional punctuation (if you don't there should be no capital letters); longer pauses and false starts should be shown; non-standard pronunciations can be shown using adapted spelling although you may wish to use phonetic transcription for these words; utterances that are unclear can be shown as 'indecipherable'. Suggestions for analysis:

■ pragmatics/functions
■ verb tenses and tag questions
■ the way in which Katharine recounts experience
■ child-directed speech.

Exam question

Here is an examination question followed by a student's answer and examiner's comments:

The extract gives examples of typical utterances spoken by children aged two and children aged three. Discuss what this data illustrates about the language abilities of children of these ages and how their ability has developed between the ages of two and three.

Age Two	Age Three
Teddy on floor.	You put that on there.
That stuck now.	Me got lots of cars like Jimmy.
Mummy gone out.	Mummy want me to go in the garden.
No daddy go.	Where you going with that red shovel?
Open it.	Daddy comed to see me in the garden.
Put in box.	I can see mummy and daddy in the mirror.
Look my dollie.	Mary went in the Wendy house with me and Paul.
What doing it?	Why you do that for?
Fall down car	Can me put it in like that?
My mouse eating.	It doesn't go that way, it goes this way.

[AEB Question 13, Paper 1, 1996]

Student's answer

At the age of two most children are at the stage known as the two word stage. Extract F illustrates the abilities of a two year old. This particular child (**1**) shows an example of negation (**2**) as he/she recognises (**3**) negatives: "No daddy go". The two year old child also shows examples of deixis because he/she uses pronouns to replace nouns: "That stuck now".(**4**)

The main sentence mood this child uses is declarative because he/she is observing things and making conversation: "Teddy on floor"; "That stuck now". The child also uses a lot of imperatives (**5**) as he/she is instructing someone to do something: "Open it". One interrogative sentence is shown: "What it doing?" (**6**)

The two year old child also knows how to use possessive adjectives: "Look my dollie"; "My mouse eating".

The child knows how to say words in the present tense with an 'ing' ending: "My mouse eating. An irregular past tense is shown: "Mummy gone out". (**7**)

All of the sentences used by the two year old are simple sentences with the determiners missed out. The child of three shows the use of deixis: "You put that on there". This child is at the telegraphic stage. The main sentence moods used by the three year old are declarative sentences: "Me got lots of cars like Jimmy"; "Mummy want me to go in the garden". The three year old also uses a lot of interrogative sentences: "Where you going with that red shovel?"; "Why you do that for?" The three year old gives commands shown by the use of imperative sentences: "You put that on there". (**8**)

Unlike the two year old, this child tends to use many pronouns: "You put that on there"; "Me got lots of cars like Jimmy". Sometimes the child says 'me' instead of the first person pronoun 'I' because he/she does not completely understand how to use pronouns yet. (**9**)

The three year old child understands how to form a regular past tense with the 'ed' ending but tends to use this ending for irregular past tenses which is Gill (**10**) Berko-Gleason's theory known as analogy. The child over-generalises one rule: "Daddy comed to see me in the garden."

Compound sentences (**11**) are shown in the three year old's language: "Mary went in the Wendy house with me and Paul". The three year old does not miss out all of the determiners.

The use of adverbial phrases are shown in the three year old's vocabulary: "Daddy come to see me in the garden"; "Mary went in the Wendy house with me and Paul". (**12**)

The child knows the rule of how to end a plural with the letter 's': "I got enough of those apples now". Also the child knows how to use abbreviations: "It doesn't go that way, it goes this way". (**13**)

As shown in extract F, a child's ability develops quite a lot between the ages of two and three. The child begins to use pronouns, understands how words are made into plurals, and understands how to form regular past tenses. At three years old the child has learnt how to use compound sentences with a continuer unlike the two year old child. The three year old child has learnt how to use abbreviations.

Examiner's comments

1 Assumes that the utterances come from one child (which they do not). Shows the importance of reading the question carefully.

2 Does not build on 'two word stage' but moves onto another topic.

3 'Recognises' should be 'uses'. It is also more important to say how negatives are formed at each age.

4 This paragraph is very fragmented, as if the candidate has not planned the answer.

5 The data suggests nothing about the frequency of these utterances. Mistake arises from the assumption in **1**.

6 There are several missed opportunities for explaining how the moods are constructed.

7 'Past tense' should be 'past participle'. Needs to connect with inflections in general.

8 Again the moods are correctly spotted but needs to put the two ages together and comment on typical development.

9 Connect this with typical development of pronoun usage over the two ages.

10 Jean.

11 Misunderstands that 'and' links 'me' and 'Paul', not two **clauses** and so the sentence isn't **compound**.

12 **Adverbials** are correctly identified but should be highlighted and connected with development of clause elements.

13 Implies that the child is deliberately abbreviating and misses changes in formation of negative.

Overall comment

The candidate understands and accurately describes many of the features shown in the data, making clear use of quotations. The short paragraphs indicate weak organisation and underdeveloped points. The comments are not rooted firmly enough in knowledge of typical linguistic abilities at these ages although the candidate knows which features are important.

Grade: D/C

ACTIVITY 55

Write a plan for the above question and then write the essay, basing improvements on the examiner's comments.

Commentary on Activity 39

The conversation in fact ends like this:

Father: Oh, you want me to sing. Sorry, I thought you were say . . . you were saying 'king'.

What this shows is that babies' utterances are often so phonologically imprecise that a fair amount of guesswork is often involved.

Children first begin to put words together at about the age of 18 months and this marks the beginnings of grammar. This chapter traced development from 'the two word stage' through to the 'telegraphic stage', focusing on acquisition of some specific features (pronouns and bound morphemes). It also considered the uses to which children put language, emphasising the ways in which children construct their own rules in a series of stages common to all children.

Recommended reading:

Child Language, Jean Peccei, 1994, Routledge.

Children's Reading and Writing, Katharine Perera, 1984, Blackwell.

5 Learning What Words Do

'... it is unlikely that a new born baby or child under one year realizes that the sounds that come out of people's mouths "stand for" things and actions.'
(Aitchison, 1987, p 89)

This chapter will consider babies' early vocabulary, the nature and meaning of their first words and some of the causes of variation, and their early pronunciation.

It's easy to believe that a baby's first word is a miraculous occasion – the moment of entry into the unique world of human beings. Parents are overjoyed that at last (it takes about one year for this to happen) their offspring has moved from crying and babbling to their first real word. And, of course, the word itself, and who or what it refers to, take on major historical importance – to be reported back to the child for English Language classes in later years.

Unfortunately it isn't quite like that. First words are difficult to identify and rather than happening at a discrete moment their emergence is best regarded as a process taking several months. Even more frustrating is the fact that even when it sounds exactly like a real word you still don't know if it really is one. Not only has the baby got to get the sounds approximately right but she's also got to mean it! So 'mamamama' may sound like the baby has worked out the name of a parent but it's just as likely to be part of the babbling that precedes speech.

Attaching labels

The first problem faced by the infant would seem to be how to attach a string of sounds to an object, person or an event in the environment. But in fact there is an even more basic problem than this. You have probably had the experience of going to a foreign country and hearing the locals talking around you. Even when you speak a little of the language they seem to speak incredibly quickly and it's impossible to work out when one word ends and the next begins. Similarly, it has been shown that in normal speech there are actually no physical gaps between words. If speech is presented graphically, using a **spectrogram**, it becomes clear that the sounds of separate words run into each other, so that in terms of sound patterns across time there is no such thing as a word. As we saw in chapter 3 adults help by emphasising and repeating certain words when they talk to babies but for the most part babies are on their own.

Even if we assume that a string of sounds has been isolated as a word, the feat of discovering its exact referent is still to be marvelled at. Steven Pinker explains why:

> 'A rabbit scurries by and a native shouts, 'Gavagai!' What does 'Gavagai' mean? Logically speaking, it needn't be 'rabbit'. It could refer to that particular rabbit (Flopsy, for example). It could mean any furry thing or mammal ... It could mean scurrying rabbit, scurrying thing, rabbit plus the ground it scurries on, or habitat for rabbit-fleas. It could mean the top half of a rabbit ... or 'It rabbiteth', analogous to 'It raineth'. The point is that the baby has to select the correct referent for the word from an enormous range of possibilities.'

(The Language Instinct, 1994)

Before looking in more detail at just how babies discover the meanings of words, it is as well to decide on what exactly we mean by 'words'.

What is a word?

ACTIVITY 56

Discuss the following criteria for a word and choose the one you think is best:

as long as the adult understands it, it's a word;
a word has got to sound like the adult version;

a word combines context and 'correct' phonology;
a word is any repeated sound;
a word has to be intentional.

COMMENTARY

A word is any sound or set of sounds that is used consistently to refer to some thing, action or quality (Bee, 1997). What this suggests is that the first word doesn't have to be recognisable as an adult word. It is more important that it functions as a word than that it sounds strictly like one. In fact it is highly likely that for the first few words the baby will not be aware that words stand for things – she will simply be aware that in certain situations what she says will have particular effects on people, getting certain reactions from them, for example.

ACTIVITY 57

In pairs discuss which of these examples you would count as a word, giving your reasons.

1 A baby says 'da' every time he hits his toy duck against the side of the bath.
2 A baby says 'dada' one day when his father enters the room.
3 On looking into a mirror an infant exclaims 'baba!'.
4 On looking into a mirror, looking at a photograph album and various books an infant exclaims 'baba!'.
5 You show a baby a picture of a gorilla in a book. She shouts 'Agh!'.

New words

Imagine a time when all words were new. A few moments' thought about the number of words that must fly past a baby in one day will indicate the vast possibilities for discovering new words. When we speak of 'new words' we mean both the ones actually produced by the baby and the ones he understands. So here we move into the realm of words that can safely be regarded as words, leaving aside problems of definition for the moment.

What are children's first words and how do they learn them? The emphasis is usually on production rather than comprehension mainly because it is a great deal easier to study the first words produced than the first words understood. Parents talk to their babies right from birth and are constantly on the look-out for signs of response. The difficulty with studying comprehension is that babies often respond to the context – features like tone of voice, the object being waved in front of them, how the adult is behaving towards that object, and so forth. So the sound of the word being uttered is often only one of a collection of cues that the baby responds to.

Speech production may be much easier to research but there is some controversy over whether or not first words are more likely to be nouns or verbs. Common sense probably suggests that nouns are easier – words like 'doggie', 'poo', 'pussycat', 'ball'. Verbs, after all, involve something happening *to* something and therefore require the baby to think about more than one idea at the same time. But the evidence is by no means clear cut. Several studies, including **cross-cultural research**, have found that well over half of the early words are nouns, whereas some recent work has found a much lower figure than this.

The content of these early words obviously varies from child to child and depends a great deal on what is talked about at home, what kinds of toys the baby has and who looks after the baby. But there are some general principles. For example, in the lists that follow, 'nappy' and 'sofa' do not appear even though they were undoubtedly part of the babies' everyday experiences.

ACTIVITY 58

■ Here are the first 50 words of two American children.

1 Sort the words into noun, verb or other words.
2 Put the words into semantic categories such as 'names of animals (probably toys)'
3 What kinds of word meanings do not appear in the lists? You should consider the size of the objects, whether or not they are handled by babies, movement and noises made.
4 Put forward a hypothesis to explain children's first words based on your analysis of this data.

Daniel: light uh-oh wassat wow banana kitty baby moo quack cookie nice rock (noun) clock sock woof-woof daddy bubble hi shoe up bye-bye bottle no rocky (verb) eye nose fire hot yoghurt pee-pee juice ball whack frog hello yuck apple Big-Bird walk Ernie horse more mummy bunny my nut orange block night-night milk

Sarah: baby mommy doggie juice bye-bye daddy milk cracker done ball shoe teddy book kitty hi alex no door dolly wassat cheese oh-wow oh button eye apple nose bird alldone orange bottle coat hot bib hat more ear night-night paper toast O'Toole bath down duck leaf cookie lake car rock box

(C. Stoel Gammon and J. A. Cooper, *Journal of Child Language*, 1984, Cambridge University Press)

Research babies' first words by:

1 recording babies between 12 and 18 months of age; and
2 asking parents of babies of that age.

You might also try asking parents of much older children to remember. Questions you should ask are: What were the first 10 words? What did they mean? In what situations were they used?

Comparisons between **1** and **2** might reveal which feature more prominently – nouns or verbs or perhaps other kinds of word – or it may be that nouns are simply more memorable than other words.

The above activities will have hinted at why babies pick up some words and not others. But the question of exactly how they learn them remains to be answered. Are babies, for example, taught new words by their parents? Is it possible that parents unwittingly reinforce all new words by repeating and emphasising them in their own speech? Are they simply the most frequent words that the baby overhears? Do they continue to learn words at the same rate? Some of these questions will be answered in a general sense in chapter 7. The extract below from a BBC radio documentary shows how linguists have tried to uncover the exact mechanism for learning new words using experimental techniques. But before reading the extract try the following activity:

Discuss in a small group how nouns might be learned in a different way from verbs. Consider these two scenarios:

1 Kashia is 14 months old. She can already say a few words such as: dadda, pussycat, guitar (pronounced 'tar'), octopus (pronounced) 'pus'. Her father is teaching her 'frog'. 'What's this Kashia? It's a frog. Yes. I'll give you the frog. (Gives her the toy frog). Now you give me the frog. (Holds out his hand). Can you say "frog", Kashia? Say "frog".'

2 Bryn is 16 months. Again he already has a vocabulary of quite a few words, including 'ball'. Bryn is in the garden with his father. He can just about stand up and walk on his own. His father is trying to encourage interest in football: 'Let's play football, Bryn. Daddy's got the ball. Daddy's kicking the ball. Oh, Bryn's got the ball. Kick the ball, Bryn! Kick the ball!'.

Extract from *Natural Genius*: BBC Radio 4

Presenter: Meanwhile with slightly older children, one of the big questions is how they go on to acquire words. [*tape of extract from mother and child*] . . .
    Mother: What about a chicken? What does a chicken do?
    Child: Chkchkchkchk . . . chkchkchkchk
    Mother: chkchkchkchk. And what's a bear do?
    Child: Bah!
    Mother: Big one?
    Child: Bagghh!

Presenter: The first 50 or so words are learned, as John Locke puts it, by brute force. Each one seems to take an agonisingly long time to master and requires understanding adult encouragement [*pause 1 second*]. So what happens next takes many first time parents by surprise. All of a sudden, a few months into the second year, the child seems to get the idea and starts to come out with all sorts of new words at an incredible rate. In fact, it's been calculated that they're learning around nine new words a day, and this continues for several years. Some new learning mechanism has obviously been switched on, and how this works is something that fascinates researchers like Professor Linda Smith of Indiana University . . .

Linda Smith: To learn words that rapidly means that they must often learn a word from hearing it used just once. Someone's got to point out to . . . a tractor and say, 'That's a tractor,' and the child has got to know from that moment forward what tractors are and if you think back on your own observations of children, that's what it seems like. You're with a child one day, you point out a novel object like a tractor, say, 'That's a tractor.' The next day you're with them, they see a slightly different brand, colour, different, longer and they say, 'tractor.' So the question is how do they know from hearing a word once what it means?

Speaker 2: You can't really, if you're trying to test this, use real words because you don't know how much experience a child has had of a word like 'dog' and 'animal' and so forth. So what researchers do is invent words like 'dax' . . . could exist in English but it happens not to, or 'bittron' and what they do is they teach children a new word like this and then they see how they extend that word to other things that are either related in colour, in shape or in category to see what sort of hypothesis the child has about what words refer to . . . [*1 second pause*]

Linda Smith: So what I have here is a dax. It looks a little bit like a early Russian satellite, kind of round with square things protruding from it and it's clay and round and it's goldy. So we say to the child, 'See this. This is a dax,' and we let the child play with it and we name it, 'this is a dax . . . this is a dax,' then we'd show them other objects . . .

Presenter: Ian, who's 22 months old, is one of her guinea pigs.

Linda Smith: So [*noise of child in the background*] what he does is he comes in and he plays with the objects in each category and we'll ask him what other things he thinks are daxes [*noises of child. LS says, 'What else?' and then, 'Is that a big dax?'*] What you do find is that children who are older than 24 months and very robust by the time they're 36 months systematically say that all the objects that are the same shape as the one we've shown them is a dax [*voice of child saying 'big dax'*].

Presenter: . . . But still, these are all words which the child has been taught. Mike Tomasello of Emery University in Atlanta is more interested in the words the child gleans less directly.

Mike Tomasello: Western children do learn a number of object labels by having adults stop and name things for them like in a picture book where adults are naming all kinds of hippopotamus and elephant that children have probably never even seen and they learn these names in this naming game, but many other kinds of words they don't learn in that same situation and it requires them to do some more active tuning into the adult's intentions in order to find out what exactly it is they're talking about. For example, adults don't name actions for children. They engage in actions and they talk about them as they're happening. So, for example, take a word like 'give': adults don't look at something happening across the room and tell their child, 'Look, there's giving. There's an example of giving.' They will look at the child and tell the child to give it to me. Or they will perhaps announce, 'I'm gonna give you this.' So children need to understand the adult's intentions in a situation where the adult is not stopping what they're doing and giving a little language lesson in naming things.

Linda Smith refers to a time about half way through the second year when children experience what is called '**the naming spurt**'. The explanation for this has nothing to do with sudden enthusiasm on the part of parents or biological programming. During the first few months of naming, babies are 'learning what words do' according to Katherine Nelson. Suddenly the point or purpose of words becomes clear and so babies realise that there must be a lot more out there that they must get their mouths around. This change is illustrated very clearly by the case of Helen Keller, who was born deaf, dumb and blind. For her this breakthrough came late and so she was able to reflect on it many years later. Her teacher held one hand under a stream of water and on the other hand spelt out the word 'water'. The revelation that words could stand for ideas and real things changed the course of her whole life.

ACTIVITY 61

1 Using the radio script and anything else in this chapter for information, create part of a website on children's first words. This would probably be part of a larger site on children's early development or on language development. Your audience is parents, the general public but not academics or researchers. The site needs to be attractive, accessible and clear.

   a Find similar websites and analyse their structure, language, audience, etc. Do this by carrying out a search on key words.

   b Sketch out your site on several pieces of paper, bearing in mind that whilst attractive presentation has advantages, it is not an art competition. It is possible to do a very good job with simple but clear sketches.

2 Using the radio script as a model, create a script for your own radio programme on any aspect of language acquisition covered in this book. You will also need to research the beginnings and endings of BBC Radio 4 documentaries. Bear in mind that parts of your script will in fact be spontaneous comment (as in the case of Linda Smith above) in which case you should write a summary of what the speaker would say.

3 Try out some of the techniques for investigating over-extension referred to in the script. It would be easier to work with pictures rather than objects.

In recent years research has compared children from different cultures. Such research allows linguists to test how universal their findings are. When differences between cultures are found this often points to environmental influences on first words such as which family members are typically present and how they address the baby.

ACTIVITY 62

Below are some samples from the early vocabularies of babies from England and China (translated into English). Sort out the words into naming and non-naming words for each nationality and then compare the kinds of words used. How would you describe the function or form of the other words in the lists?

English girl		Chinese girl	
run	dog	Momma	not want
Mommy	no	grandmother	flower
juice	moon	go	noodles
all gone	book	Papa	cooked rice
more	want	come	uncooked rice
Daddy	kitty	lamp	afraid
babar	dolly	wall clock	thank you
baby	bye-bye	pick up	chicken
	eye		horse

(Bee, pp 222–223)

COMMENTARY The two lists contain roughly the same number of naming ('mummy', 'juice') and non-naming words ('afraid', 'thank you'), with most of the words falling into the former category. This suggests that nouns dominate early words irrespective of the culture in which a child is raised. The non-naming words are sometimes verbs ('not want', 'go'), sometimes adjectives ('more', 'afraid') expressing basic actions and feelings. Ritualised farewells ('bye-bye') and politeness ('thank you') also begin to show the management of social relationships.

Over and under-extension

Linda Smith described an example of children's extensions of meaning in the radio script above. That is, she illustrated how, based on a single example, children extend meaning to other objects, and this is the process of generalisation that remains part of the process of learning new words throughout our lives. However, a well-known feature of young children's language is that they **over-extend** meanings, so, for example, 'daddy' might initially be any male who happens to walk into the room! In recent years more attention has been given to **under-extension** – when a baby restricts the number of referents of a word, usually to the original context in which the word was learned. For example, if 'white' refers only to snow. A second kind of under-extension occurs when the meaning of a word is narrower than usual, as when a child uses 'clock' only to refer to a wall clock and no other.

Babies sometimes over-extend on the basis of shape, as we have seen, but is this always the case? Here are two hypotheses that attempt to explain the basis of over-extension:

1 **The semantic features hypothesis**
   This means that the baby over-extends on the basis of the features that combine to give an object meaning, for example, colour, shape, sound, movement, etc. So any moving thing with four legs could be called 'cat'.
2 **The functional similarities hypothesis**
   Here over-extension results from similarities in the uses to which objects are put. Things used to hold liquid might all be called 'cups'.

Be careful when you assume that over-extension has something to do with the way babies think – that they are dominated by shape, colour or the sound an object makes, for example. It may be that they simply do not know the word for something, so babies do what we all do – use the nearest word they know.

ACTIVITY 63

1　In pairs discuss what might be happening in the following example:
Two year old Zoe has a male doll. She has recently seen her mother bathing two month old Jacob. The next day she points to the doll's genitals saying 'poo'. Soon after all dolls are called 'baby Jacob'.

2　Design an investigation to test the two hypotheses suggested above.

3　Why do you think under-extension is more difficult to study than over-extension? Explain to someone else how the cartoon in Figure 3 below works.

Figure 3

'That's a cloud, too. They're all clouds.'

Drawing by Gahan Wilson; © 1984
The New Yorker Magazine, Inc.

Doing things with one word

The so called one word stage, which lasts until approximately the age of 18 months, is also sometimes called the **holophrastic stage**. 'Holo' means complete and so the implication is that one word stands as a complete phrase or sentence in itself and is therefore able to do the job of more than just a single word.

ACTIVITY 64

Challenge yourself by choosing a single word (for example, *ball*) and testing it against Dore's functions on page 49 to see how many it can achieve on its own. Then move on to adult functions like persuade, advise, protest, instruct, inform, explain, question, entertain, etc. Given the right context, how far can you go with just one word?

COMMENTARY   The difference between you and a baby is that you have a choice. Babies
don't and so they use holophrases because they have no other way of
making their message more explicit. Babies use holophrases extensively at
first, although, as we saw on page 48 they are initially limited in the
number of functions they can perform with language. For example,
Halliday believed that babies do not use language to inform until they get
to nearly two years old. Here he meant 'inform' in the strictest sense and
not in the sense that crying means 'I am informing you that I am hungry.'

ACTIVITY 65

The list below gives holophrases and the
contexts in which they occurred.

1 Cover up the right hand column and suggest
   possible meanings for the words given.
   Experiment with different ways of saying
   them.
2 With a partner compare your answers and
   then decide how these meanings would be
   limited by the contexts given on the right
   hand side.

'Up'	The baby raises his arms whilst sitting in his high chair.
'Up'	Mother is sitting down, baby standing in front of her.
'Milk'	A glass of milk has been upset.
'No'	A spoonful of mashed carrot is hovering in front of the baby.
'Mummy'	Mummy has entered the room.
'Mummy'	Mummy is listening to 'The Archers' on the radio.
'Birdie'	Daddy has said, 'Who gave you that then?'
'Birdie'	Daddy is making the toy bird 'fly' across the room.
'Uh oh'	Teletubbies is on television.
'Uh oh'	A glass of milk has been upset.

COMMENTARY   As we have seen in previous chapters meaning-making often requires two
people, especially when the baby is at the one word stage. Holophrases are
therefore very dependent upon adults making a **rich interpretation** of the
baby's utterances – that is, going beyond what is immediately obvious from
the utterance itself.

ACTIVITY 66

Draw a chart giving several of your own examples of over-extension and holophrases. With a partner write a short paragraph

explaining the difference between the two. You might need to re-read some of the foregoing sections to do this.

Developing vocabulary

ACTIVITY 67

Once children have over-extended a word how do they come to use it with the adult meaning? When they hear new vocabulary and understand it well enough to incorporate it into their own usage, what happens to the word they already used for that thing? The table below shows how the semantic field of animals could

develop in a child over a number of years. Work out the principle behind the over-extension and how each new word might be distinguished from the others. Explain to a partner how children learn the terms in a semantic field.

The stages are Brown's (see page 3).

	Word	Referents
Stage 1	bow-wow	dog(s)
Stage 2	bow-wow	dogs, cows, horses, sheep, cats
Stage 3	bow-wow	dogs, cats, horses, sheep
	moo	cows
Stage 4	bow-wow	dogs, cats, sheep
	moo	cows
	gee-gee	horses
Stage 5	bow-wow/doggie	cats, dogs
	moo	cows
	gee-gee	horses
	baa	sheep
Stage 6	doggie	dogs
	moo	cows
	gee-gee/horsie	horses
	baa lamb	sheep
	kitty	cats

(based on Eve Clark, 1973, in Lee)

COMMENTARY   The table shows that when children use a new word, like 'cow', it replaces one of the meanings of 'dog' instead of running along beside it. 'Cow' must then be distinguished from the other words in that field, probably through sound or shape (large with horns). At the same time children stop over-extending the other words in the same semantic field. Eventually children stop distinguishing on the basis of one or two features (like shape, colour, sound, etc) and grasp the whole idea of a cow, for example. Some researchers have suggested that children seem to know that most words are not like 'this' and 'that' – the meaning of which changes depending on what they refer to – and secondly that, on this occasion, they know that a cow is not a type of dog.

As a result of the research into the development of vocabulary, some linguists have suggested that progress falls into three distinct stages. Again they are really describing production whilst assuming that comprehension works in roughly the same way but a little in advance. Much of this amounts to a summary of what we have seen so far in this chapter.

- **Stage one**: the baby begins to respond consistently to words but is highly dependent on context.
- **Stage two**: after a few months the baby has worked out what words are for and acquisition of new words speeds up dramatically so that babies are now capable of **fast mapping**.
- **Stage three**: from about the age of three or four, word-learning becomes even faster. Children at this stage are re-organising the way they categorise words; for example, they can now put things into more than one category at the same time, so that something can be both a dog and an animal at the same time.

One word styles?

In discussing babies' early vocabulary it is easy to make the assumption that all babies are the same. And when there are differences we tend to say things like, 'it varies from individual to individual' without really explaining why babies differ. Research by Katherine Nelson suggested the possibility that babies can be divided into 'types' according to how they learn new words. She identified two 'styles' : **referential** and **expressive**. The following table sums up the differences in the two styles:

Referential	Expressive
Early words linked to objects	Early words linked to social relationships (eg, greetings)
high proportion of nouns and adjectives	low proportion of nouns and adjectives
few formulae	many formulae ('What do you want?)
no inflections (eg, -ed endings) at stage 1	inflections at stage 1
more telegraphic	

(table from Bee, p 242, based on Thal and Bates, 1990)

ACTIVITY 68

Apply the ideas in the above table to any of Katharine's dialogues in this book. Is Katharine referential or expressive?

Dowboys and Indians: phonological rules

You might have got the impression from reading this chapter that babies' production of words is a black and white thing: either words are not recognisable or they are perfectly formed words. But this is far from the case. In fact most of the examples that have been given assume a less than perfect articulation. Even when babies have started to produce what sound like recognisable words, many of them are not pronounced like those of adults. You have probably heard babies saying things like 'goggy' instead of 'doggy', and will be familiar with completely new words that have become established features of babytalk, such as 'geegee' for 'horse'. An important question is whether these deviant pronunciations are purely random or are they in some way systematic? And if they are systematic, that is, governed by a rule or a series of rules, why has that system developed in the way that it has? Babies may simply be unable to get their mouths around the complexities of pronunciation or another possibility is that they do not hear speech as adults do. Keep these issues in mind as you do the activities:

Here are the systematic ways in which babies' pronunciation differs from that of adults:

deletion: often when an adult word ends in a consonant, a baby will simply miss out the consonant, as in 'ca' for 'cat' and 'bi' for 'bib'. In words of more than one syllable the beginning of the word is more likely to be deleted than the end.

substitution: this is where the baby actually substitutes one sound for another. For example, when 'cat' becomes 'tat'. Often babies will avoid consonants that involve friction (the 'sh' in 'ship') in favour of one involving a stopped sound (the 't' in 'top'). So 'ship' might come out as 'tip', or it might be simplified to 'sip'.

addition: this often involves the addition of an extra vowel sound to the end of a word. So, adult 'egg' might be pronounced as 'egu' by a baby.

de-voicing: this is the process of taking the voice out of /b/ to produce /p/ (try whispering /b/ to feel the difference). Babies prefer de-voicing at the end of words, so 'pig' might become 'bi<u>k</u>'.

voicing: the opposite of the above. At the beginnings of words babies are more likely to voice an unvoiced consonant, as in '<u>p</u>ig' becoming '<u>b</u>ik' (see activity on page 76).

assimilation: this happens when one consonant or vowel becomes similar to another, as in 'gog' for 'dog'.

reduplication: this refers to the repetition of a whole syllable, as in 'choo-choo'. This has become a recognised feature of 'babytalk'.

ACTIVITY 69

For each of the examples below work out which of the above processes applies bearing in mind that there could be more than one for each.

1 Dat's a circle.
2 Me want nother bissie.
3 A baby says 'bootoo' for 'button'.
4 'Glue' becomes 'goo'.
5 'Chocolate biscuit' becomes 'cocker bisik'.
6 A baby called Francis attempts to say his own name. It comes out as 'Sassy'.
7 **Baby**: Put dem down 'ere (there).

8 **Mother**: Which one have you got?
   Baby: A snowowman
9 'Want do bano'. What do you think the baby is trying to say here?
10 Many children say 'mama' for 'mummy', 'tummy' for 'stomach'.
11 'Little' becomes 'iku'.
12 'Wing a wing a woses!'
13 **Baby**: He's standing on the ephelant.
14 'Raindrops' becomes 'raindops'.

ACTIVITY 70

The beginning of James Joyce's novel, *A Portrait of the Artist as a Young Man* is influenced by the language of a young baby:

'Once upon a time and a very good time it was there was a moocow coming down along the road and this little moocow that was coming down along the road met a nicens little boy named baby tuckoo ...'.

1 Identify the features of a baby's language that Joyce incorporates into his text.
2 Write the beginning of an autobiography in which you imitate some features of the way in which a baby speaks. You might include: phonological features and babytalk; telegraphic speech; asking questions; negatives; vocabulary, etc. Don't forget to keep the text readable.
3 You might like to develop your text into the first part of an autobiography, taking it up to about the age of 4 or 5. Change the language to suit the age of the baby. This could be developed into a piece of coursework.

The above rules explaining babies' pronunciation seem clear cut enough but they tend to over simplify. Clearly the rules are only tendencies and not every word uttered by a baby will obey them. In addition there are further complications associated with comprehension and production. These are illustrated in the following activity:

ACTIVITY 71

What does the sequence of events below suggest about the relationship between a child's production and perception or comprehension of language?

Roger Brown was speaking to a child who referred to a 'fis' meaning 'fish'. Brown replied using 'fis' and the child corrected him but again saying 'fis'. Finally Brown reverted to 'fish' to which the child responded, 'Yes, fis.'

A baby says 'dowboy' instead of 'cowboy' without realising it. But he can hear his parent say 'cowboy'.

(based on *Learning to be Literate*, Garton and Pratt, 1989)

COMMENTARY Clearly babies do not hear themselves in the same way that they hear others and no amount of correction will change this. Their pronunciation cannot be explained fully by not being able to articulate certain sounds. The 'th' in 'thin' is more difficult than 'b' but babies can often produce a sound in one word but not in another. For example, they might say 'moush' for 'mouse' but then produce 'sip' for 'ship'.

This chapter has been concerned with babies' early vocabulary – the problems faced when entering the world of words, the nature of babies' first words and their meanings, some of the causes of variation and their early pronunciation. Some research biases have been identified: an emphasis on production rather than on comprehension, and a tendency to look for systematic similarities rather than differences between babies. It is worth remembering that babies' pronunciations are often unlike those of adults. Not only do they require knowledge of the context in which they were uttered but they are also constantly changing.

Recommended reading

Words in the Mind: An Introduction to the Mental Lexicon, Jean Aitchison, 1987, Blackwell.

Child Language, Jean Peccei, 1994, Routledge (for phonological development).

The Emergence of Language: Development and Evolution, William S-Y Wang, 1991, Freeman and Co.

6 Learning the Tune Before the Words

'Because she was the baby
she couldn't walk, and she couldn't talk.
But she could cry.'

(A Lion in the Night)

In this chapter we will explore the non-vocal and then the vocal aspects of the first year, looking back towards the possibility of pre-natal learning about language, before considering in the last chapter, the extent to which language is in our genes.

It is tempting to assume that language learning begins with the first word but this is far from true. Babies typically utter their first word at about the age of one year but a great deal has happened before that time. There is, for example, much that babies can understand: they have learned, for example, about English phonemes (see p 76) and intonation patterns and thus we can say that they learn the tune before the words. But they also know a great deal about the social situations in which language works – that, for example, conversation requires people to take turns. So, in that case, where does language begin?

A note on terminology is probably needed at this point. **Pre-verbal** refers to anything that the baby does or says before meaningful words are used; **non-vocal** refers to behaviour that does not involve the voice; **vocalisations** refer to sounds made using the voice but which cannot be described as words.

Conversation without words: routines and turn-taking

The infant's daily routines help considerably in language learning. Such routines make language predictable and, more importantly, they allow language to refer to objects that are physically present for the baby; for example, when playing with rattles and other toys. These situations also help the parents, as shown by Trevarthen and Richards who videoed five babies over the first six months of their lives. They found that from the age of six weeks the babies' hand movements, facial expressions, voice tone and lip movements are different when their mothers are talking to them. Mothers in turn respond to these apparent features of turn-taking and so conversation is sustained. In other words babies are treated as if they have intentions like real conversational partners. Research has also shown that as babies get older, parents respond to different aspects of their behaviour. At first, **gaze** is important – the parent works out where the baby is looking and comments on the object. Later the baby's actions serve the same purpose and a few months after that, actions are combined with words.

Some researchers emphasise the importance of non-vocal interaction (eg pointing, turn-taking, joint action) between parent and baby, especially in the first year. They believe that what you can do at first without words comes to be done later with words. So, for example, when the baby points it is like saying 'Look at that!'. Harris et al (1995) found that pointing coincided with babies' first understanding of object words. Turn-taking in a game where the adult and then the baby takes a turn, later becomes turn-taking using language – which is the basis for conversation. More will be said about this in the next chapter as it represents an important theory of language acquisition.

ACTIVITY 72

In the following examples of parents' responses to a three and a half month old baby write down the assumptions made about the causes of their baby's behaviour. Say which pairs might contribute to language learning and why.

Baby	Parent
smiles	Who's a happy boy then?
looks sideways	What you looking at?
sneezes	Ooh!
passes wind	Ooh, that wasn't very nice, was it?
vomits	Oh, didn't you like it?
urinates	Not on me!
kicks legs	Be careful. You'll shoot off the end.
holds rattle	Good boy.
puts rattle to mouth	That's a clever boy.
cries	He's not in a good mood this morning.
looking at object	He really likes that elephant grass.
looking at mother	Hello!
burps	That's a big burp.

ACTIVITY 73

1 In pairs brainstorm routines that parent and baby might share during a day.
2 For each one suggest baby activities that might count as responses for the parent, for example crying during nappy-changing might be seen as the baby objecting.
3 Using one of these routines write a

monologue with pre-verbal contributions from the baby. You could make this into an annotated example of child-directed language for the leaflet in activity 28 on page 32.
4 Develop a monologue in the style of Alan Bennett's *Talking Heads*, based on an adult talking to a baby.

Vocalisations

The pre-verbal stages

The pre-verbal stages provide an outline of vocal development during the first year. Like all stage theories they should be treated with caution as babies vary a great deal, the stages are sometimes difficult to distinguish and different researchers use different terms, sometimes to refer to the same thing.

ACTIVITY 74

The order of stages given below is random (based on Crystal, 1986). With a partner, decide on the correct order using the brief descriptions given. Justify your answers then read the detailed notes below. The answer can be found at the end of the chapter.

1 **Vocal play** A controlled single vowel-like or consonant-like sound. More varied than babbling but much less controlled.
2 **Biological noises** Vomiting, coughing, burping, crying, a low cooing sound, etc. These are common to the whole human race: there are no Icelandic burps or Thai cries.
3 **Melodic utterance** Melody, rhythm and intonation develop. Parents assume that these sounds have different functions: questioning, exclaiming, greeting etc. Babies of different nationalities sound increasingly different from each other.
4 **Babbling** The baby produces phonemes, often in the form of combinations of vowels and consonants (eg ma, ga, ba, baba, gaga). These sounds are largely those that appear in the child's native language.
5 **Cooing and laughing** Produced when the baby is in a settled state. These are short vowel-like sounds. 'Quieter, lower-pitched and more musical than biological noises' (Crystal 1986). Some consonant-like sounds come from the back of the throat. The baby is beginning to develop control over the vocal muscles.

Crying

Crying is the most important of what are sometimes called vegetative noises – noises associated with various basic activities such as feeding and being sick. It is the most important because for the first few weeks of life it is the main indicator of the baby's basic needs. Unless they are brain damaged, crying is the same for all babies. There are different kinds of cry, indicating: pain, hunger, discomfort. The baby's cry is the first sign that the baby wants something although it is not clear that the baby can communicate exactly what is wanted. There is some evidence that at about three or four months the parent is able to distinguish between different kinds of cry: pain and hunger, for example. However, it is perhaps not so much the variation in the baby's cry that allows this as the context in which the cry occurs. For example, preceding events such as sleep, time since last feed and nappy changing will affect the likelihood that a hunger cry has occurred. These features will affect the parent's interpretation of the cry. As with other aspects of young children's communication adults are left doing most of the hard work. This is how difficult it can be:

ACTIVITY 75

Invent your own categorisation of the mother's interpretations of Paul's crying in the extract below. What assumptions does she make about the meanings of his cries?

Paul: age 6 months: [**Paul** *is sat alone in the middle of the living room. He starts to cry* **Mother** *comes into the room.*]

Mother: Oh, now what's up, hey? Oh dear, Oh dear, what's the matter? [*She picks him up.*]

Mother: Are you thirsty, is that what it is? Do you want a drink? [*She goes and picks up his bottle and offers it to him. He refuses it and continues crying.*]

Mother: Hungry? Are you? Do you want something to eat? No? Sleepy then, do you want to go to sleep? [*She puts him in his pram but he continues to cry. She picks him up again and walks about comforting him. She stops at the window. Paul apparently looks out but continues crying . . .*]

Mother: Look, there's a pussycat, can you see him? Do you know what pussycats say? Do you? They say 'miaow' don't they, yes, of course they do. [*Paul stops crying during this speech.*]

Mother: There, that's better, down you go then. [*She places him back on the floor.*]

(From Andrew Lock, 1978, p 43)

COMMENTARY

For about six months after birth cries are interpreted as having physical causes, as in the case of Paul and his mother above. After that time parents begin to assume underlying psychological causes and so their responses to the baby change. Here Paul's mother eliminates a number of physical causes before attempting to build on the present context – Paul's looking out of the window. She then begins to assume that his cries must be aimed at attracting her attention and so she engages Paul in conversation about what he might be looking at. The fact that Paul then stops crying suggests that she has finally got it right. A few weeks later the cry begins to become more ritualised or conventional. This means it has become less of a reflex and more of a means of communication. There is a sense that there is a growing intention behind the cry; the baby now seems to pause as if checking for an adult response, and the cry itself is less persistent. The baby seems to know that this is the kind of stuff that gets things done! All of this happens before the baby is able to say exactly what he wants. This is important because the baby seems to be learning about the purposes of language before the forms.

In later months, perhaps up to one year and beyond, crying can be combined with other gestures such as pointing, raising arms and lip-smacking. For example, crying might act as an attention-grabbing device, pointing indicates who is to perform an action, and lip-smacking shows exactly what is wanted (food!). Some scholars believe that this combining of gestures to create meanings mirrors what happens later with words. The baby also learns that gestures can be used to refer to things (lip-smacking refers to food or eating). Once this has been achieved the infant is half way towards realising that words can also refer to things (Lock, 1978).

Crying is followed by cooing and laughing and then vocal play, although, of course babies continue to cry – usually for far too long. The most significant stage is the next one – babbling – since it is often used to characterise a typical pre-verbal utterance.

ACTIVITY 76

Design an investigation to find out:

1 whether or not people can distinguish different kinds of cries;

2 if parents are better at this;

3 if people believe there are different kinds of cries.

Babbling – what are the rules?

This stage is perhaps the one you are most familiar with and the one that has attracted the most attention from experts. The popular view is that babies babble before they can speak. It is surely no coincidence that 'baby', 'babbling' and 'babababa' are all remarkably similar in their basic sound. At one time experts believed that babies babble all possible sounds of the world's languages. This is no longer regarded as true although initially the range of sounds is wider than those of the child's native language. Another myth is that babbling stops and real words take over; for some babies this is true but others will continue to babble several months after their first words.

ACTIVITY 77

The rules of babbling

Below are listed some of the different kinds of sounds that make up babbling; they are in approximate rank order from easiest to most difficult. Note that babbling consists of consonant-vowel combinations.

EASY   **stopped sounds** – where air is momentarily stopped from being released ('p')

reduplication – where the same vowel-consonant combination is repeated

variegated babbling – as above except that the vowel sound changes

consonant cluster – where a number of consonants are combined, as in /fr/

DIFFICULT   **friction sounds** – where there is vibration whilst air is released (the 's' in pleasure)

1 Identify the above sounds in the examples below.

2 Suggest why some combinations might be easier than others and propose an approximate rank order of ease of articulation.

splocka babababababa adu bpbpbpbpb taba dadudaduda shugushugu

Proto-words

Generally speaking, proto-words are what come in between babbling and adult-like words. We have already seen that babbling consists of a consonant vowel consonant vowel pattern, such as bababa or dadada. Proto-words can sound exactly the same as this although there might also be more difficult combinations like 'gigl' (which has nothing to do with the adult word 'giggle'). What is important is that proto-words seem to function as words even though they do not sound exactly like them. So you would expect to hear the same sound in a variety of situations, used for the same purpose. For example, Halliday's son, Nigel (see page 48) made a sound like 'door' to mean 'look, that's interesting.'

Comprehension of sounds

ACTIVITY 78

1 With a partner practise saying /b/ and /p/ taking it in turns. Try to describe the difference. Repeat this several times.
2 Now try whispering the same two phonemes to your partner. In a predetermined order whisper either /b/ or /p/ about ten times. Can your partner guess which is which?

What do you notice? What difficulties are there in trying to distinguish the two?
3 On your own hold your hand up close to your face as you say 'spot' and then 'pot'. What do you notice about the /p/ sound? Does this difference create any difference in meaning?

COMMENTARY   /b/ and /p/ are phonemes in English. That is, the difference between them creates different meanings in the words that use them. So, 'bong' means something different from 'pong' because of the different phonemes at the beginnings of these words. /b/ and /p/ are largely distinguished by the amount and timing of the voicing – that is, whether or not your vocal chords actually vibrate as you say them. It should have been easier to whisper /p/ than /b/, and whispering (which gets rid of the voicing) should have made the two difficult to distinguish. The final exercise shows that the /p/ phoneme in 'spot' and 'pot' is not exactly the same in both cases. In 'spot' you should have noticed less breath against your hand – less **aspiration** of the /p/. However, this difference doesn't actually create any difference in meaning – that is provided by the presence of the 's'. In fact, most of the time we don't notice the degree of aspiration although in some languages of the world it would make a difference.

As with many aspects of language acquisition it is important to consider how the baby learns to distinguish the sounds discussed above. Are they learned through listening to adults or is the baby pre-programmed to be able to make certain distinctions? In fact babies can tell the difference between /p/ and /b/ at a very young age and as a result many languages feature these two phonemes. However, some distinctions are less common, like the one above between the two kinds of /p/, and do have to be learned through listening, if a language requires it. If a language does not use the distinction to make a difference between the meanings of words then the speaker of that language will lose the ability to make that distinction. So, for example, some languages do not distinguish /p/ and /b/ which means that infants gradually lose the ability to distinguish these sounds as they become adults.

How do we know these things? Babies are plainly unable to communicate this information to us and so ingenious techniques have been developed by psychologists: sucking harder on a dummy can indicate that the infant has distinguished between two sounds, or turning a head can mean that one voice has been recognised over another. For example, it has been shown that two month old babies can distinguish between the /th/ of thin and the /f/ of fin. Some experts have argued that this is evidence for an **innate** language ability but the same ability has also been shown to exist in some monkeys. So perhaps such incredible ability to discriminate sounds is just a built in part of our auditory system.

But the role of learning must not be underplayed. Ann Fernald has shown that five month old babies will smile more when they hear adults talking in approving tones as opposed to disapproving tones, irrespective of the language being spoken. English babies also prefer to listen to English words that have a typical English stress pattern, with the stress on the first rather than the second syllable (for example, pencil, table). These findings demonstrate how babies are constantly learning from a very young age about intonation and stress patterns.

ACTIVITY 79

Peter, a few hours old, appears to be fascinated when his bi-lingual father suddenly speaks to him in French. Discuss whether this reaction is just wishful thinking on the part of the father or if there might be a genuine reason for it.

Pre-natal development

ACTIVITY 80

Consider how you might explain the facts that recent research has uncovered:

- At birth babies can tell the difference between speech and non-speech.
- They have a preference for language as opposed to other noises.
- Three day old infants can distinguish the voice of their mother from other voices.
- An eight month old foetus will respond differently to familiar compared with unfamiliar rhymes (De Casper, 1994).
- Newborn babies prefer their own language to others.

COMMENTARY There is currently a great deal of evidence that language learning begins in the womb. This should come as no surprise: in more and more spheres it has become evident that a mother's experiences affect her unborn child. Why should language be any different? It is highly likely that babies can pick up the intonation patterns of their mother's voice through the womb wall, mixed with other biological noises such as digestion and heart beat. Intonation also seems to be a significant factor after birth. Experiments have shown that muffling the consonants used by parents has no effect on recognition of the native language, whereas playing the tape backwards – which upsets the intonation but not the consonants – interferes with the baby's recognition.

You might have considered that the evidence given for pre-natal learning in fact suggests certain innate abilities. This debate will be dealt with in chapter 7.

The role of pre-linguistic behaviour in language acquisition can be reduced to a number of statements:

- Babies turn-take before they can speak.
- Non-vocal behaviour such as pointing and shared attention may lead directly to language.
- Routines are a useful context for language learning.
- Parents often assume intentions on the part of their babies, based on pre-verbal behaviour.
- Non-vocal behaviour combines with vocalisations in important ways.
- Babies go through a fixed series of vocal stages in their first year.
- Babies are born with impressive abilities to discriminate the sounds of language, some of which are innate, others of which are probably learned in the womb.

Answer to Activity 74

earliest to latest – biological noises; cooing and laughing; vocal play; babbling; melodic utterance.

Recommended reading

Early Language: The Developing Child, De Villiers and De Villiers, 1979, Fontana.

Language Development, Andrew Lock and Eunice Fisher, 1984, Routledge.

7 How Do They Do It? – Theories of Language Acquisition

Throughout this book we have presented suggestions as to how children acquire particular aspects of language. But there has been no overall answer to the 'why?' question at its most general: why is all of this possible? Or to put it another way, what are the underlying psychological, biological or social reasons for children's initial language development?

ACTIVITY 81

Discuss with someone else your personal feelings about the causes of language acquisition, either on the basis of ideas gained from this book or using your own ideas. Do you consider language acquisition to be:

■ primarily pre-programmed (innate)?
■ learned through imitation of what babies hear around them?
■ highly dependent on the development of the ability to think?
■ supported by adults in various social contexts?
■ Do you think one theory could explain all aspects of language development? Is language acquisition explained in the same way at different ages?

The expanding circle of theories of language acquisition

Beginning with Chomsky, theories of language acquisition can be thought of in terms of an expanding circle, beginning in the middle and moving outwards towards the present day.

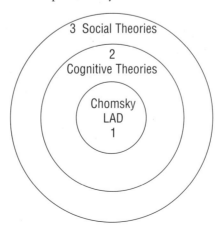

This model suggests how theories of language acquisition have changed their focus:

- from one highly specialised mechanism (1);
- to the whole person (especially the development of intelligence) (2);
- to the role of other people (3).

This chapter traces the development of these theories, beginning in the middle of the diagram.

The Big Two

Noam Chomsky appeared at the centre of the picture in the late 1950s largely in response to the work of B. F. Skinner. Skinner was a psychologist determined to apply his philosophy to every aspect of human and animal behaviour. He started by studying pigeons pecking levers for rewards and then began to apply his thinking to humans. That philosophy was **Behaviourism** – the belief that all behaviour is conditioned (basically punished or rewarded) by experience until it becomes automatic. In the case of language babies imitate their parents and are rewarded or punished according to their accuracy. This meant that, for Skinner, biology played almost no part.

Very shortly after the publication of Skinner's book *Verbal Behaviour* in 1957, Chomsky, a linguist, replied with a blunt attack on Skinner's work. He argued that language acquisition was largely innate. One of his main reasons for claiming this was that the language that children experience is **impoverished** – it is incomplete in the sense of being a small sample of language and it is grammatically flawed as parents do not speak in complete sentences in the run of everyday conversations. In short, children could not possibly learn language by copying what they hear. Much of Chomsky's own work was concerned with describing the complex grammatical rules which explain how humans produce language. It was left to others to apply his thinking to children.

Today Skinner's ideas can be largely dismissed without a more detailed consideration of his work. However, it would not be wise to deny that imitation and parental encouragement, two important mechanisms for Skinner, do have some part to play. Much depends on which aspects of language are being considered. Two of the lasting effects of the Skinner-Chomsky debate are: firstly there is a tendency to think that you have to choose between one or the other, when in fact there are several other positions available; secondly it is easy to forget that language has many facets, each of which might require a different theory to explain it. For example, imitation plays a more important part in phonological development than it does in grammatical development. A further complication is that the way in which language is learned may change from stage to stage.

The caution we should adopt towards Skinner and Chomsky is perhaps best summed up by psychologist George Miller who said that Skinner's view was 'impossible' but Chomsky's 'miraculous'. Let us now consider Chomsky's ideas in more detail.

ACTIVITY 82

Before thinking about Chomsky's ideas, try these activities:

1 In pairs make up meaningful utterances that you know you have never said before. Discuss how it is that you are able to do this.

2 How many meanings can you find for this sentence? Try showing them in terms of the clause elements.

Time flies like an arrow (clues: *fruit flies like a banana; how do you time those flies?*)

COMMENTARY

The first activity should have been astoundingly easy – there are thousands of things you have never said before and you will continue to say new things throughout your lives. This would be true even if you never learned any more vocabulary. So how is it that you are able to do this? One answer is that you have **linguistic competence** – you know the underlying rules for producing meaningful utterances in English and so the new things that you say obey those rules. In this sense language is creative – we can produce an infinite number of utterances using a limited set of rules.

What do we mean by rules? This brings us to the second question. The sentence 'Time flies like an arrow' can refer to: how quickly time passes, how to time flies (if they were racing) and the thing that 'time flies' (if you can imagine such a species) prefer. You put these different meanings together by breaking up the sentence into different units, all of which are allowable within the system we know as English. These two concepts – competence and rules – are important for Chomsky's theory of language acquisition.

Chomsky

You should remember that Chomsky has changed his ideas many times since they were originally formulated in the '50s and '60s, and the influence of these early ideas is the main focus here. Chomsky was concerned with the rules for producing language – the underlying knowledge that makes language possible. In the same way, chess players need to know the possible moves and the constraints on these moves before they can actually play chess. To continue the analogy, Chomsky was much more interested in these rules than he was in actual games of chess. In terms of language he was less concerned with the real utterances produced by people, with their false starts, and various accents, than he was with the rules that made those utterances possible. In other words he studied the language of an **idealised speaker**, based on his own intuitions about English. He didn't carry out any investigations and never studied real children – this gives an idea of how far removed his ideas were from language as it is performed by real people. But his philosophy triggered off a wealth of experiments amongst a whole generation of psycholinguists.

Throughout this book we have seen that children are surrounded by examples of language in use. Chomsky proposed that children combine this information with the knowledge of language that they already have in their heads. It is the latter that Chomsky regarded as being innate. This innate knowledge was part of **The Language Acquisition Device** or **LAD** (a term coined by McNeill) which has knowledge of what Chomsky called **linguistic universals**.

Linguistic universals

These refer to the features that all languages have in common, such as nouns and verbs. Chomsky claims that babies are born with an innate knowledge of these universals and this speeds up their learning of their native language when they hear it. This is a bit like travelling to a foreign country, hearing the language and knowing in advance that some words will refer to 'things', some to 'actions'. Note that children can't have knowledge of any particular language at birth because they are able to pick up any language with equal ease. An innate knowledge of Mandarin would certainly give this language an advantage over English. So babies must know the basic rules behind *all* languages, bearing in mind that these rules are buried somewhere inside the head. The LAD works using something like the following sequence:

1 The baby already knows about linguistic universals.
2 The baby hears examples of language in its native language.
3 The linguistic universals help the baby to make hypotheses about the incoming language, for example: That grunt is irrelevant; those words always have *-ing* on the end.
4 From these hypotheses the baby works out a grammar, a set of rules – see, for example, the two word grammars on page 43.
5 As more and more language is heard the grammar becomes more and more like that of adults.

ACTIVITY 83

The abstract nature of Chomsky's theory means that analogies are particularly useful aids to understanding. Discuss the following analogies, making connections with the foregoing descriptions of Chomsky's work.

1 According to Chomsky in what ways is a pianist waiting to sight-read a piece of music like a child learning language? (Aitchison, 1989).

2 In what ways is a child like a scientist?

Beyond Skinner and Chomsky

Chomsky emphasised what children must already know rather than the effect of the experiences they have whilst growing up. Many researchers followed suit by investigating in a practical way the things that Chomsky had only speculated upon – children's knowledge of grammatical rules. However, the idea of impoverishment (parents' language is 'insufficient') prompted others to look in more detail at language experience, with an emphasis on social circumstances and the language of adults. This leads us to some of the most important work of the last 20 years or so.

More recent research emphasises social or experiential factors on the one hand, or cognitive factors on the other. The latter proposes that language development parallels the development of thinking and knowledge and was originally associated with the work of Jean Piaget, a Swiss psychologist. This will be covered first.

Piaget believed that language is to a large extent controlled by the development of thinking. This seems to make sense. If a baby can use sentences involving phrases such as 'more than', 'less than', 'as much as', it is obvious that the concepts of 'more than' etc must have been grasped.

ACTIVITY 84

With a partner or in a small group discuss the likely outcomes of the following two experiments.

1 Children of about seven were taught phrases like 'more than', 'less than' etc to see if they had any beneficial effect on their ability to grasp these concepts in a practical activity involving water. What happened? Did the phrases help the children to grasp the concepts?

2 An important aspect of Piaget's theory is that children achieve object permanence before the age of two. This means that they know objects continue to exist even when they can't be seen. Did children's grasp of the word 'gone' appear after the development of object permanence as Piaget would predict?

COMMENTARY

In 1 the language tuition did not seem to help, suggesting that children must mature into these concepts and then use of the appropriate vocabulary will follow. In 2 'gone' in fact seemed to appear at about the same time as object permanence. 'Gone' may therefore help children to understand object permanence rather than the other way round. Much of the evidence concludes that the strongest links between cognition and language occur at the very earliest stage. However, probably the firmest nail in the coffin of this theory comes from growing evidence that for some children there is a complete mismatch between thinking ability and linguistic ability. There are cases of children who are capable of fluent, grammatical nonsense and others whose speech is impaired but whose intellectual ability is not (see Genie on p 86).

Bruner

If the cognitive theorists realised that language acquisition was related to the development of the whole child, those who emphasised social aspects extended their theory to take account of other speakers (see the expanding circle on p 79). Bruner puts language acquisition firmly into a social context, emphasising that language gets things done: 'Children learn to use a language initially . . . to get what they want, to play games, to stay connected with those on whom they are dependent.' (1983, p 103)

Partly as a humorous response to the LAD, Bruner proposed the existence of **LASS – The Language Acquisition Support System**. This system essentially refers to the support for language learning provided by parents – who do more than provide models for imitation. The example below illustrates this.

LASS and shared reading

Parents often use books as a focus of attention for developing babies' naming abilities. This can also show how parents offer a support system for their children's language learning. Note too how the baby doesn't only learn the names of objects and actions but also needs to know rules for participating in this kind of conversation. In other words the baby doesn't learn names for their own sake but learns them as part of a naming activity with its own social rules. Recent research (Whitehurst, 1988) has found that if parents use specific teaching strategies their babies' language development can be significantly improved.

Bruner found a four phase structure in a mother's interactions with her child while sharing a book – an example of the LASS provided by the parent.

1 Gaining attention – drawing the baby's attention to a picture
2 Query – asking the baby to identify the picture
3 Label – telling the baby what the object is
4 Feedback – responding to the baby's utterance

Some variation was observed when the baby correctly named the object (phase 3 was either missed out or coincided with feedback).

ACTIVITY 85

1 Sort the following examples of utterances used by mothers into the four types described by Bruner (these are Bruner's typical examples):

What's that?	It's not an X	Isn't it?
What does that do?		
It's an X Look!	We'll call it an X	What do you
see there?		
Look at the X	No, it's an X	Yes
Look at that!		

2 Now try applying the same types to some real data. Katharine and her mother are discussing *The Snowman* by Raymond Briggs. (This is on the accompanying cassette). Consider:

a What problems there might be in applying Bruner and how you might adapt his framework.

b Any other strategies used by this parent to support learning.

Tape Extract 6

(*The vertical line indicates overlapping speech*)

M: So what's this book about?
K: Snowman.
M: Mmm. What's the snowman doing?
K: 'S flying.
M: Mmm. Who's he flying with?
K: James.
M: James. Yes.
K: Making he body.
M: He's making his body, yes. And what's he putting on there? (1) On the top of the body he's put the …?
K: [*indecipherable*]
M: The what?
K: Head.
M: The head, yes.
K: Hair, hair.
M: He hasn't got any hair, has he. Poor snowman hasn't got any hair but he's got a hat, hasn't he.
K: He's got there hat. Dat one's sleeping.
M: Mmhuh.
K: [*indecipherable*]
M: What's
James made his nose out of?
K: Uh, orange nose.
M: Orange. Yes, it's an orange nose.
K: Yeh.
M: Let's have a look. What's he doing? Ho, ho, ho, ho! He's coming into the house. And what's he doing there? He's trying all different noses. What's he trying there?
K: Pinenose.
M: Pineapple nose, yes.
K: He's got no nose.
M: Yes, he's got a pineapple nose and there he's got no nose.
K: He's got it [*indecipherable*] on back again. He's got it on back again.
M: He's got it on back again, yes, yes. He's got his orange back on again. Mmm.

ACTIVITY 86

Set up your own investigation into the language used by adults interacting with babies whilst sharing a book. The situation needs to be interactive rather than just the adult reading the story to the child. Try to use Bruner's categorisation system, note any variation in the order or frequency of the categories and develop your own categories if necessary.

ACTIVITY 87

In small groups create a chart or spider diagram containing the names of the major theorists and their key concepts as presented in this chapter. Then discuss which theory of language acquisition the following evidence tends to support:

a language learning is innate;
b cognitive theories;
c social theories;
d language is learned through imitation, reward and punishment.

1 A universal grammar is a set of characteristics that apply to all languages. For example, similar grammatical categories (noun, verb etc) exist in all languages.

2 Parents seem to **reinforce** their children's attempts to speak by showing excitement, talking back and feeding them.

3 Language is **species specific**. Attempts to teach animals language have met with limited success.

4 Lenneberg (1967) put forward the **critical period** hypothesis. This simply means that the human brain is designed to acquire language at a certain time (ie during the first five years) and that once this period has passed normal language is no longer possible. There are two kinds of evidence relating to this theory:

   a **Genie** was a thirteen year old girl raised in appallingly deprived circumstances. She was fed on little more than bread and water and kept in a locked room since birth, with no chance for interaction with others. Up until this time she had not developed language. With care and training she was able to learn some language. She could produce novel sentences (sentences she had never heard before) but never fully recovered. Do you think this supports or refutes the critical period hypothesis?

   b **Feral** or wild children. The most famous case is that of Victor, The Wild Boy of Aveyron. Victor was discovered at about the age of 12 in a French village. He could not speak and it was believed that he had been raised in the wild by wolves. In spite of extensive treatment from a young French doctor, Victor never learned to speak. Does this support Lenneberg, was the boy already retarded and abandoned by his parents or were the doctor's methods simply inadequate?

5 Clarke-Stewart (1973) found that children whose mothers talk more have larger vocabularies.

6 Many but not all cultures use special language when talking to children – Child-directed language (see chapter 3).

7 A limited set of **rules** can produce an infinite set of utterances.

8 Several researchers have found that parents often respond to the **truth value** of what their baby is saying, rather than its grammatical correctness. For example, a parent is more likely to respond to 'there doggy' with 'Yes, it's a dog!' than 'No, it's *there is a dog*'.

9 Katherine Nelson (1973) found that children who were **corrected** developed more slowly than those who were not. See also 'the fis phenomenon' (p 69).

10 There is considerable evidence that children learn language at about the same age, acquiring particular elements in roughly the **same order**. Deaf children whose parents did not know sign language have been known to create their own limited language using signs.

11 Children eventually learn to say 'went' instead of 'goed'. This seems to be learned through listening, **imitation** and correction.

12 In 1958 Berko-Gleason's famous research found that children were able to provide the plural of 'wug', the name of an imaginary creature, even though they had never heard the word before.

13 Children are capable of lexical innovation: they make up new names

for things as in 'pinenose' (= pineapple nose); 'Mommy nippled Anna'; etc.

14 Attempts to change children's utterances like 'nobody don't like me' have proved to be unsuccessful even after repeated tries.

ACTIVITY 88

Answer this exam question using information in this chapter and, in particular, chapter 3.

'As far as acquisition of language is concerned, it seems clear that reinforcement, casual observation, and natural inquisitiveness (coupled with a strong tendency to imitate) are important factors, as is the remarkable capacity of the child to generalise, hypothesise, and 'process information' in a variety of very special and apparently highly complex ways which we cannot yet describe or begin to understand, and which may be largely innate, or may develop through some sort of learning or through maturation of the nervous system.'

(Noam Chomsky)

■ Discuss, with illustrations from your own observations and study of children acquiring language what you consider to be the relative importance of social environment and of the child's innate faculties in its acquisition of language.

(Cambridge, 1996)

This chapter has considered the contributions to language development of innate factors and experience. The debate opened with the ideas of Chomsky and Skinner. Chomsky's ideas have been far more influential, spawning a wealth of research that moved a long way from his initial position. There are few people who would support a Skinnerian view of language acquisition today although much recent research has turned again towards social and experiential factors in language acquisition – particularly the part played by adults. Most modern opinions acknowledge the contribution of innate and experiential factors, with most current research examining the precise relationship between the language children hear, the social contexts in which they hear it and the process of learning to speak.

Recommended reading

The Communicative Competence of Young Children, Susan H. Foster, 1990, Longman.

Developmental Social Psychology: From Infancy to Old Age, Kevin Durkin, 1995, Blackwell.

The Language Instinct, Steven Pinker, 1994, The Penguin Press.

The 1996 Reith Lectures, Jean Aitchison.

Glossary

ADDRESSEE 'The person or group of people being addressed by a text.

ADDRESSER This refers to the person in a text who seems to be addressing the reader. It often but not necessarily refers to the writer.

ADJACENCY PAIR These are pairs of utterances that go together usually in spoken language. For example, questions and answers.

ADJECTIVE An example of a word class. Adjectives describe nouns and appear before nouns or after the verb 'to be' (examples: 'big', 'happy').

ADVERBIAL An example of a clause element. It is the element which answers the question 'how', 'when', 'where', 'why' when asked of the main verb of the sentence. For example, in 'She loved him always,' the adverbial is 'always' because it answers the question 'when?'.

AFFIRMATIVE SENTENCE The opposite of a negative sentence. For example, 'I am hungry'.

AGENT An agent is responsible for performing an action in a sentence. For example, in 'The fruit was eaten by the girl,' the girl is the agent.

ARTICLE An example of word class. For example, 'The, a, an'.

(TO) ARTICULATE The physical act of producing language, to put into words.

ASPIRATION The amount of breath put into a sound.

BOUND MORPHEME This is a meaningful part of a word that cannot stand on its own as a word. 'Antidisestablishmentarianism' comprises five bound morphemes and one free morpheme – 'establish'.

CLAUSE Traditionally a group of words containing a verb, such as: 'After going to church…', 'They eat puffins.'

CLAUSE ELEMENT Sentences can be broken down into the clause elements: subject, verb, object or complement, adverbial.

CLOSED QUESTION This is a question that usually takes a yes/no answer or another limited set of alternatives.

COMPOUND SENTENCE This is a sentence containing two clauses linked by 'and', 'but' or 'or'. For example, 'She went to town and bought some books'.

CONTENT WORDS These are words that carry the main meaning of a sentence, such as nouns, verbs and adjectives. They are usually contrasted with function words.

COMPREHENSION Usually contrasted with production in language acquisition. It refers to the act of understanding or perceiving language.

CONCRETE NOUN A noun that refers to a tangible object rather than an idea or concept. Usually contrasted with abstract nouns.

CONTEXT An important term in language study. It can refer to the situation in which language appears, who is present, what has just happened or the language surrounding a particular text or word.

CONTEXT DEPENDENT Context dependent language requires an understanding of the context in which it appears in order to fully understand it. For example, pronouns: 'he', 'she', 'it' etc.

CROSS-CULTURAL RESEARCH This is research that compares children's language acquisition in more than one culture, concentrating on significant similarities and differences.

DEIXIS (DEICTIC) Deictic words are ones which 'point' to objects in the world, such as 'this' and 'that'. To fully understand them the context in which they are used must be grasped. 'Tomorrow' is deictic because you have to know when the speaker is using it to know which day is being referred to.

DIRECTIVE This is language that gets someone to do something. It often refers to commands but questions can also be directives as in 'Would you mind switching on the light?' Instructions are also directives.

ELLIPSIS This refers to words that have been missed out because they are assumed by speaker and listener. For example, when someone is asked where they are going and they reply 'to town', there is no need to say 'I am going'.

FIELD Sometimes called semantic field, it refers to a topic in which the items have some association with each other. For example, knife, fork, dinner, salt, etc.

FUNCTION This is the more technical word for the purpose of an utterance.

FUNCTION WORDS Not to be confused with the above. This is the collective term for words which do not refer to things but have only a grammatical function in a sentence. Roughly this means anything which is not a noun, verb, adjective or adverb.

GAZE This refers to the act of looking at and attending to something usually for a prolonged period.

IMPOVERISHMENT This was Chomsky's term for inadequacy of parental input to children's language acquisition. He did not mean that people do not speak properly any more! He simply meant that every day language is often incomplete and fragmented.

INFLECTIONS These are parts of words that show some grammatical function like past tense (-ed), or plural (-s).

INNATE   Anything which is innate is present from birth and is presumed to be biologically programmed.

INTERACTIVE TEXT   An interactive language situation is one in which both participants can respond to each other. Most written texts are not interactive although they can give the impression of being so by asking questions.

INTONATION AND STRESS   The intonation of an utterance can be determined by factors like which word is stressed or whether or not the pitch rises or falls. For example, rising intonation often indicates a question.

LEXICAL WORDS   These are sometimes called **content words** because they carry the main content of a sentence (for example, nouns and verbs). They are often contrasted with grammatical or **function words** (for example, articles).

LINGUISTIC COMPETENCE   Chomsky's term for a person's underlying knowledge of linguistic rules. It is the knowledge that enables people to create new sentences.

LOOK AND SAY   A method of teaching young children to read that emphasises the context of language (for example, the use of pictures) and the shape of whole words. It is usually contrasted with **phonics**.

MODAL AUXILIARIES (MODALS, MODAL VERBS)   These are parts of the verb that suggest probability, possibility or permission. For example, 'I might mark those essays'. They usually indicate a person's attitude towards the action in question.

MODE   Refers to speech and writing and the various hybrids that come in between, such as writing which is designed to be spoken aloud, such as a radio script.

MODIFIER   These are words that usually come before a noun in a **noun phrase**. They are frequently adjectives ('the big match') but can be other nouns ('lunch time').

MORPHEME   The smallest part of a word that has semantic content. For example, 'unhappy' breaks down into two morphemes.

MORPHOLOGY   Refers to the study of **morphemes**.

NOUN PHRASE   This is a collection of words that centres around a noun (the head word) with words sometimes appearing both in front of and after the head word. For example, 'The lonely shepherd with his hands in his pockets'.

OBJECT   A **clause element** that answers the question 'who' or 'what' if placed after the verb.

OBJECT PERMANENCE   This is a psychological concept that refers to a young baby's ability to understand that the world and the things in it continue to exist when you can't see them.

OPEN QUESTION   This is a question with many possible answers. It is usually contrasted with a **closed question**.

PASSIVE In passive sentences the usual order of elements is reversed. The thing that receives the action is brought to the beginning of the sentence and the **agent** appears at the end. For example, 'The ball was kicked by the boy'.

PAST PARTICIPLE This is the part of the verb that comes after an auxiliary like 'have' or 'is'. For example, 'I have eaten'. It is often different in form from the past tense. For example, 'I ate'.

PHONEME This is the smallest unit of sound that makes a difference to the meaning of a word. The degree of aspiration of a sound is not a phoneme in English but a long or short 'a' can make the difference between 'cat and 'cart'.

PHONICS This refers to the teaching of reading using the traditional method of associating letters with sounds.

PHRASAL VERB Phrasal verbs have another word after them without which the meaning would be different. For example, 'to put up with'; 'to come over' (all dizzy); 'to go off'.

PRAGMATICS This is the study of the way that language functions in society, often with unspoken rules for communication. A child with perfect grammar but with no knowledge of pragmatics would not know what language is used for and would be a very sad person.

PRE-LINGUISTIC This is usually the time before the baby's first word is uttered.

PRE-NATAL Before birth.

PRODUCTION Language production refers to a person's language output – spoken or written – as opposed to their comprehension. Not to be confused with original writing which is referred to as 'language production' in some exam syllabuses.

READING SCHEMES Sets of reading books that are graded in sequence according to the ability of the reader.

REAL BOOKS These are contrasted with **reading schemes** and refer to books written by individual authors outside any particular scheme.

REPRESENTATION When anything in the real world is converted to linguistic form it is said to be represented in language. The issue is usually the degree to which a representation is biased. For example, the words in the English language representing women are biased against them.

RE-LEXICALISATION This is when a text replaces a word with another that means roughly the same thing at a later point in the text. For example, when 'man' is replaced by 'guy'.

SEMANTICS This is the study of linguistic meaning or the meaning of words. In the field of language acquisition semantic development looks at how children's meanings differ from adults'. For example, When a child uses 'dog' to mean any animal with four legs.

SEMANTIC FIELD (see **field**)

SPECTROGRAM   This is a computer-generated graph that provides a visual representation of sound.

STAGES   In language acquisition studies a stage is a period in a child's development characterised by certain linguistic features. Gordon Wells offers this advice: '… referring to "stages" is nothing more than a convenient way to describe the child's development. In fact, this development is more or less continuous, with no sharp boundaries between successive stages.' (1986, p 21)

SUBJECT   One of the **clause elements** found by asking the questions 'who?' or 'what?' before the main verb of the sentence.

SYNTAX   This refers to the rules for combining words in English.

TAG QUESTIONS   These are question units that appear at the end of statements. They reverse subject and verb as in: 'These are Paul's books, aren't they?'

TENSE   This is the time referred to by a verb, as in 'past, present or future'.

TURN-TAKING   This refers to the tendency for people in conversation to take turns to speak. Linguists are interested in uncovering the rules that govern this behaviour.

UNANALYSED   If you referred to an 'unmanned' (unpersoned?) space craft and then later to a 'manned' spacecraft, it would be assumed that you were aware of the **morphemes** 'un' and 'manned' that make up the word. Someone who uses 'unmanned' but never any variation on that word might be unaware of its construction and is therefore using it in an unanalysed way.

VERB   One of the **clause elements** from which the others can be found. Traditionally verbs were called 'doing words' although many of them do not 'do' much: to be, to have, to seem, to wonder, to hope.

VOICING   This refers to the vibration of the vocal chords to produce the difference between 'z' and 's'.

BARTON PEVERIL
COLLEGE LIBRARY
EASTLEIGH SO50 5ZA